Learning Functional Programming
Managing Code Complexity
by Thinking Functionally

Jack Widman, PhD

Beijing · Boston · Farnham · Sebastopol · Tokyo

Learning Functional Programming

by Jack Widman, PhD

Published by O'Reilly Media, Inc., 1005 Gravenstein Highway North, Sebastopol, CA 95472.

O'Reilly books may be purchased for educational, business, or sales promotional use. Online editions are also available for most titles (*http://oreilly.com*). For more information, contact our corporate/institutional sales department: 800-998-9938 or *corporate@oreilly.com*.

Acquisitions Editor: Mary Preap	**Indexer:** nSight, Inc.
Development Editor: Shira Evans	**Interior Designer:** David Futato
Production Editor: Kate Galloway	**Cover Designer:** Karen Montgomery
Copyeditor: Justin Billing	**Illustrator:** Kate Dullea
Proofreader: Stephanie English	

August 2022:   First Edition

Revision History for the First Edition

2022-08-11:   First Release

See *http://oreilly.com/catalog/errata.csp?isbn=9781098111755* for release details.

978-1-098-11175-5

[LSI]

To my three wonderful daughters: Katherine, Annie, and Victoria. And to Andrea, whose support and love have encouraged me in so many ways.

Table of Contents

Preface

Over the past few years, functional programming (FP) has been experiencing a renaissance. Many companies are looking for programmers with experience in FP, as languages that were not originally designed to be functional have evolved over time to include functional capabilities: languages such as Java, JavaScript, and Python, to name a few. The push for programmers with functional experience is due, in part, to a perceived improvement in the development process, including a sense that fewer bugs are produced and more extensible and robust code is produced when following the functional way. Whether this is true or not—and whether a greater percentage of the code written in the coming years is functional—will become evident in time. For now, let us consider FP one of a number of paradigms, each with its own pros and cons.

Who Should Use This Book?

Essentially, all programmers. If you have no experience in FP, but have heard about it and you are curious, or even if you picked up this book in a store without any knowledge of FP, this book will prove useful to you. Experienced FP programmers too, will find something to benefit them. The book dives into the category theory roots of FP in a way not presented in other books on this subject. Finally, programmers with some experience using FP but who want to gain a more advanced understanding of the concepts and theory that make up FP will find much to use and enjoy.

How The Book Is Organized

I endeavor to demonstrate, through various programming languages, how functional constructs can improve our code. However, you will notice that Scala is the frequent language of choice for code examples due to the ease with which functional ideas can be expressed in Scala; the reader will more easily appreciate and understand the functional ideas when they are expressed in the natural way, which Scala allows. For a mini-introduction to Scala, see the Appendix.

Conventions Used in This Book

The following typographical conventions are used in this book:

Italic
> Indicates new terms, URLs, email addresses, filenames, and file extensions.

`Constant width`
> Used for program listings, as well as within paragraphs to refer to program elements such as variable or function names, databases, data types, environment variables, statements, and keywords.

 This element signifies a tip or suggestion.

 This element signifies a general note.

 This element indicates a warning or caution.

O'Reilly Online Learning

 For more than 40 years, *O'Reilly Media* has provided technology and business training, knowledge, and insight to help companies succeed.

Our unique network of experts and innovators share their knowledge and expertise through books, articles, and our online learning platform. O'Reilly's online learning platform gives you on-demand access to live training courses, in-depth learning paths, interactive coding environments, and a vast collection of text and video from O'Reilly and 200+ other publishers. For more information, visit *http://oreilly.com*.

How to Contact Us

Please address comments and questions concerning this book to the publisher:

O'Reilly Media, Inc.
1005 Gravenstein Highway North
Sebastopol, CA 95472
800-998-9938 (in the United States or Canada)
707-829-0515 (international or local)
707-829-0104 (fax)

We have a web page for this book, where we list errata, examples, and any additional information. You can access this page at *https://oreil.ly/learning-fp*.

Email *bookquestions@oreilly.com* to comment or ask technical questions about this book.

For news and information about our books and courses, visit *https://oreilly.com*.

Find us on LinkedIn: *https://linkedin.com/company/oreilly-media*.

Follow us on Twitter: *https://twitter.com/oreillymedia*.

Watch us on YouTube: *https://youtube.com/oreillymedia*.

CHAPTER 1

What Is Functional Programming?

Functional programming? Functors? Monoids? Monads? "I'm not a mathematician!" you might say. How can I learn these esoteric concepts? And why would I want to? These concerns are totally understandable. But the truth is you don't need to be a mathematician to be a functional programmer.

The fundamental concepts of FP are easy to understand when presented in a clear, straightforward way. And that is what this book is about. Making FP understandable and practical. In particular, I will teach you how to *think* like a functional programmer. But why would you want to learn FP?

Picture this. It's 10 p.m. and you are totally stuck while trying to fix a bug in a program you need to submit in the morning. The problem seems to be centered around a variable called *ratio*. The problem is that depending on the state of the system you are modeling, the variable ratio keeps changing. Your frustration builds. Or you have a deadline at work and there is an elusive bug in your microservice that you are chasing down. The problem seems to be in two nested for loops in which variables are modified in a fairly complex way. The logic is complex and you don't quite see the solution. If only there were a way to write programs in a way in which the value of variables would not change! FP to the rescue.

 Variables whose values change often are a considerable source of bugs in programs. It can be difficult to keep track of the value of the variable since it can change at any moment.

So, what is FP? What makes one language functional and another not functional? The truth is that to some extent it is a matter of degree. You don't have to follow every principle that falls under the heading of FP. Some people will try to follow all of them, and others will pick and choose. It is totally up to you. FP is a paradigm, an approach to programming, a way of breaking up the world and putting it back together in code. It involves both how we organize that piece of the world we are modeling and how we organize and structure the code.

To better describe the essence of FP, let us begin by contrasting it with imperative programming and object-oriented programming (OOP). There are others, such as logic programming, but the three mentioned are by far the most popular.

Imperative is what you might think of as plain old programming. It's what programming was before OOP and FP. In imperative programming, you write functions or procedures, use for and while loops, and mutate state often. Languages like C or Pascal are typical imperative programming languages. Then there is OOP. Currently the most popular paradigm, OOP is a process of modeling the world as a collection of objects. Each object has state and methods, which are operations representing behaviors specific and relevant to that object. As the program runs, the state of the objects changes. The benefits of this approach include encapsulation, which means the state and methods that belong to an object exist, at the code level, within the object. This is a much better idea than letting the state be scattered all throughout the code because managing mutable state is just plain difficult. You have multiple variables and their values are changing. The approach of FP is to acknowledge this and attempt to minimize, if not erradicate, changing state altogether.

Eradicating changing state, rather than attempting to manage it, is a fundamental principal in FP.

Ultimately, it is not always possible to avoid having mutable state, so the standard FP approach is to isolate the part of the code that mutates state. When we cannot eradicate all changing state, we can at least localize the code with the changing state into one place.

Immutability

The single most important aspect of FP is immutability. Generally speaking, this means a lack of change. Something is considered immutable if we cannot modify it in some way. In FP, this means a few things. Once a variable is set, its value cannot be changed. If $x = 3$ at the beginning of a program, it has that value for the remainder of the program. Does that mean that if a program is written in a functional style, and a person's age changes, this change cannot be modeled? Of course not. That would be absurd. There are techniques like efficient copying that allow us to manipulate our code without ever mutating state. Consider the following simple for loop in Java that prints the numbers 0 to 99.

Java

```
for (int i = 0; i < 100; i++) {
    System.out.println( i );
}
```

This type of code occurs all the time. You might wonder how we could possibly express this in an immutable way. It seems that the essence of this code is the changing of the value of the variable i. A common approach in FP is to use recursive functions; a recursive function is one that calls itself. In the case of the preceding code, you can put the code in a function and then call the function on the next value of i in each iteration. It might look something like the following:

Java

```
void f(int i) {
    if (i > 99) {
        return;
    }
    else {
        System.out.println( i )
        return f(i+1)
    }
}

f(0)
```

Now this code is a little longer, but it does not mutate any state. If you know a little about FP, you might know that the return type void is a sure giveaway that there will be side effects.[1] A side effect is anything that affects the program outside of the function. Things like writing to a file, throwing an exception, or modifying a global variable. The earlier code example is meant to show a single way of avoiding the mutation of state. You have probably been mutating state your whole programming career and it likely seems indispensable. But remember two things:

- It feels very natural to mutate state
- Mutating state is a major cause of code complexity

The good news is that with practice, the FP way will feel just as natural.

---

1 In FP, all functions should return a value. void is a sure sign of side effects.

Let us consider another technique for avoiding the mutation of state. Imagine you have an object with a property or field that changes. The question here is how to model this situation without mutating a variable in the code. Let us consider a Java example first.

Java

```java
public class Person {
    private final String name;
    private final int age;

    public Person(String name, int age) {
        this.name = name;
        this.age = age;
    }


    public static void main(String[] args)  {
        Person person = new Person("Carl", 32);
        //A year passes
        Person changedPerson = new Person("Carl", 33);  ❶
        System.out.println(changedPerson);
    }
}
```

❶ Instead of modifying the value of age in the Person object, we create a new object and initialize the new age value in the constructor.

Let us now look at an example in Python.

Python

```python
class Person:
    def __init__(self,name,age):
        self.name = name
        self.age = age

    def main():
        person = Person("John",22)
        #One year later
        changedPerson = Person("John",23)
```

One year passes and we need the Person object to reflect this. But we *can't* modify the value age. So we create another immutable object with the age variable initialized to 23.

Now let's look at an example in Scala.

Scala

```scala
case class Person(name: String, age: Int) ❶
val person = Person("Katherine", 25)        ❷
val changedPerson = person.copy(age=26) ❸
```

❶ Declare a `case` class.

❷ Create an instance of the class.

❸ This line makes a new instance of `Person` and initializes age to 26. No state has been mutated.

Immutability is one of the most important aspects of FP. Having a lot of mutable state in a program results in a lot of bugs. It's simply not easy to keep track of all the changing values. Here, we have seen some examples of how to get around the apparent need to mutate state. It takes some getting used to but with a little practice, using these techniques may even start to seem natural.

Referential Transparency

The next crucial component of FP is referential transparency. We say an expression is referentially transparent if we can replace it with its value anywhere in the code. You might think, upon first hearing about this, that you can always do this. Let us consider a simple example of a nonreferentially transparent function.

Java

```java
today()
```

If I call this function, get *May 29th, 2021*, replace its body with this value, and then call it tomorrow, I will get the wrong answer. So the today function is not referentially transparent.

Here are a couple more examples of nonreferential transparency:

- A function that returns a random number. Obviously you can't replace the body of the function with a value you get when you call it once.

- A function that throws an exception. Exceptions are generally avoided in FP. I will come back to this later.

It probably seems that if we throw out all nonreferentially transparent functions (and that is what we will aim for), that we will lose some valuable capabilities—that perhaps we will be unable to express certain useful things. Rest assured, there are functional ways of expressing these things.

A related concept that you will see in writings about FP is purity. Unfortunately, there is some confusion in the literature about the relationship between purity and referential transparency and not everybody agrees on the meanings of these terms. Generally, a function is said to be pure if it has no side effects and for a given input, always returns the same output. This basically means that if the input is x and the output is y, no matter how many times you call the function with x as the input parameter, the function will return y. A side effect is anything that happens outside of the context of the function. Writing to a file and throwing an exception are two examples of side effects. Forget for the moment that we need to write to files (though arguably we don't need to throw exceptions), and think how nice it would be if every time we call a function with the same input parameters, we get the same output and nothing outside of the function is changed. *That* is something we enjoy in FP.

 In FP, we strive to use only pure functions. That is, functions that have no side effects and have the property that if you supply the same input, you get the same output.

Because different people have different views on this, and because the differences between referential transparency and purity are subtle, I will treat the two terms as synonymous.

Now, I said you don't have to be a mathematician to write functional programs, and you don't. But FP does come from mathematics. It comes from two fields, actually, lambda calculus and category theory. Category theory has much to do with functions. And in mathematics, functions are pure. When a programmer looks at an expression like $x = x + 1$, they say, "Ah, increment the variable." When a mathematician looks at $x = x + 1$, they say, "No, it doesn't."[2]

Now what would an impure function look like?

Scala

```scala
object Main extends App {
  def impureFunction(x: Int): Int = {
  import scala.util.Random
  return Random.nextInt(100) + x
  }
  println(impureFunction(5))
  println(impureFunction(8))
}
```

---

2 This is meant to be a joke, but I've experienced these reactions firsthand.

The two function calls will very likely return different output values for the same input value. This function is not pure. We have said mathematical functions are pure. Well, programming has gained quite a lot from this mathematical approach. Functional programs are clean, pure, and elegant. FP style may take a little bit of getting used to at first, but as we gradually move through the basic ideas of FP in this book, you will begin thinking like a functional programmer. Your functions will be pure and your code will be clean.

The biggest benefit, however, of writing functional programs is that you will have a much stronger expectation that your programs will be correct.

Let me make an important point here. We can't define FP with negation; we can't say it's the same as ordinary programming except that we leave out this, that, and the other thing. The hard part, the part accomplished by the many creators of FP, is how to express everything we need in a functional way.

Higher Order Functions

FP is all about functions. What we want, in a FP language, is the ability to treat functions as first-class citizens. This means we should be able to pass them as function parameters and return them from functions as return values. Let's discuss why higher order functions are an important part of FP. One key goal in FP is to get to the heart of the matter. This means we need to be able to express concepts concisely in our language. If we want to square every integer in a list, for example, we shouldn't have to loop through the list and modify each number by squaring it. We should be able simply to directly apply a `square` function to every element of the list simultaneously. The `map` function, in many languages, allows us to do this. It allows us to work at a higher level of abstraction. That higher level corresponds to a higher order function. We will see this as a major theme as we proceed.

An imperative approach:

Python

```
def square(nums):
    squared = []
    for i in nums:
        squared.append(i*i)
    return squared
```

A functional approach:

Python

```python
def square(nums):
    return map(lambda n: n*n, nums)
```

As shown in the Appendix, `lambda` is a way of creating an anonymous function; that is, creating a function without a name, or *on the fly*, as it were. The `map` function acts on members of a list and, all at once, applies it to all the elements of the list.

Lazy Evaluation

Another component of FP is lazy evaluation. This simply means an expression is not evaluated until it is needed. This is not, strictly speaking, necessary for a language to be functional but often languages that are by nature *more functional*, tend to be lazy. Haskell, for example, is lazy by default and can be thought of as the archetypical FP language. It was designed by a committee of academics and makes no compromises when it comes to functional principles. Most popular languages are not lazy, though, and use what is called *eager evaluation*. This means an expression is evaluated every time it is encountered. As you'll see in the following example, there are two benefits of lazy evaluation:

Imagine you want to define your own `if` statement. Let's call the function `myIf`. You might want to add a logging line to every `if` statement, for example. If you try the following, you will encounter a problem.

Scala

```scala
def myIf(condition: Boolean, thenAction: Unit, elseAction: Unit): Unit =
    if (condition)
        thenAction
    else elseAction
```

Can you see the problem with this definition? With eager evaluation, which most common languages have, when the function is called, the first thing that happens is that all of the parameters are evaluated. So in the case of `myIf`, both the then Action and the `elseAction` will be evaluated when you want only one of them to be evaluated, depending on the condition variable. However, with lazy evaluation, this would work. In this and related cases, it would allow you to write your own control statements.

With eager evaluation, function parameters are evaluated as soon as the function is called. With lazy evaluation, they are not evaluated until they are needed.

Another benefit is performance improvement in certain situations. Since the lazy code is evaluated only when it is needed, it is often the case that it is actually evaluated less than it would be in the eager evaluation case. This can speed up the program.

In Scala, we can use call by name parameters. In the following code, thenAction and elseAction are evaluated only when they are needed. That is, they are evaluated lazily. The following will work as expected.

Scala

```
def myIf(condition: Boolean, thenAction: Unit, elseAction: Unit): Unit =
        if (condition)
            thenAction
        else elseAction
```

With lazy evaluation, we can create our own versions of operators like if or while.

In conclusion:

- Lazy evaluation allows you to define control flow structures in your code directly as opposed to their being operators built into the language.
- It can speed up performance.

Thinking Like a Functional Programmer

In this book, we will focus on how to think like a functional programmer. While there are a wide range of approaches to FP, some concepts are universal across these approaches. Functional programmers don't mutate state, for example. That is, once a variable has been set, it is never changed. Also, functional programmers tend to use lots of higer order functions. These are functions that take other functions as parameters and/or return a function as a return value.

 To know how a functional programmer really thinks involves knowing a set of idioms, or patterns that promote functional code.

It's all well and good for me to tell you not to mutate your variables, but unless you know how to work around this, implementing immutability may not make any sense. In other words, patterns are an important part of FP.

You may have heard that functional programmers don't really care as much about patterns as object-oriented programmers do. This is a misconception. What *is* true is that the term *pattern*, in the context of FP, refers to something different than the Gang of Four patterns.[3] The Gang of Four patterns (e.g., prototype, proxy, and flyweight patterns) were developed in the context of OOP. These can largely be implemented in a functional style and are useful in the design of programs, but there is nothing particularly functional about this type of pattern. One might say they are *functional-neutral*. While the Gang of Four patterns are functional-neutral, there is another category of software patterns that is explicitly functional. These patterns, such as the functor and monad patterns, derive from ideas in category theory. We'll look at these in greater detail in Chapter 3.

The Benefits of FP

The benefits of FP are becoming clear. It aids us in our quest for bug-free code. Or as close to bug-free code as is possible. And how does it do this? By rewiring our brains so that we no longer see the world as a mass of objects, each with its own changing state and processes that transform that state. With a change of perspective, we can identify state as the culprit.

 When state changes, we need to keep track of it, which means there is more complexity to manage, and more bugs. This is problem FP solves.

Human beings can handle only so much complexity before we start writing code that isn't quite correct. "But wait," you say, "The world is made up of objects. And those objects have state, and that state changes over time! So we are right to model the world this way. That's exactly how the world is!" But that doesn't mean we can't begin to see (and model) the world in more functional terms. For now, the important thing is to realize that writing bug-free software is not something we really know how to do. I knew a computer science professor who once started off his introduction to programming class with the sentence: "The human race does not yet know how to program."

A bit dramatic, perhaps, but true. Projects typically come in above budget and take much longer than predicted. The reason is complexity. Programming is the art, science, and engineering of managing complexity. FP brings with it tools we can use in an attempt to restrain and control this complexity. Tools like immutability, referential transparency, and higher order functions, to name a few. Master these tools, and your code will be less buggy.

---

3 You can read more about the Gang of Four in *Design Patterns* (*https://oreil.ly/kH7VD*) by Erich Gamma et al. (Addison-Wesley).

FP Can Improve Productivity

So FP is a programming paradigm. What other paradigms are there?

The most popular is arguably OOP.[4] If you have programmed in Java, C#, C++, or Python, for example, you are probably familiar with this method of programming. In this case, the world is modeled as a collection of objects each with its own state and its own behavior. OOP has many benefits, including abstraction, encapsulation, and inheritance. But even with these benefits, code often suffers from coming in overbudget and overtime. Before FP and OOP became popular, there was imperative programming. On the surface, imperative programming resembles FP a bit. are the main software abstraction used in imperative programming; there are no objects or classes. But on closer inspection, one sees that state is mutable, functions are not referentially transparent, and imperative languages didn't necessarily have higher order functions. C and Pascal are two examples of imperative programming languages.

You could argue that the best programmers will produce better code no matter what paradigm they use—this is probably true. The question is: if we have two developers of equal skill, one working with an object-oriented approach and the other working with a functional approach, who will be more productive? The clarity, power, and higher level of abstraction will allow the functional programmer to produce more correct code, faster.[5]

FP Is Fun!

There is another reason to program with FP. This is perhaps the most important reason yet.

FP is fun, and for deep reasons.

FP lets you get to the heart of the matter. It lets you cut to the chase and spend more time coding on the subject matter. It is at a sufficiently high level of abstraction that it feels as if you are manipulating important, relevant concepts instead of drudging through low-level details that closely model what a machine does.

---

4 While there is more OOP code in existence currently, there is clearly a move in the direction of FP among many developers. It remains to see how this will play out. Perhaps a hybrid approach that mixes both approaches will become the norm. Or perhaps FP will just continue to get more popular.

5 To be clear, this is my opinion.

The history of programming languages, from one perspective, is largely a story of ever increasing abstraction level. The higher the level, the easier it is to avoid manipulating masses of detail. FP shows us that abstraction does not have to be difficult. Yes, there is a learning curve, but it is possible to shorten this curve by making the change little by little. If you currently code in Java, JavaScript, or Python, for example, it is possible to gradually include idioms, structures, and practices that will make your code more functional and before you know it, you will start to naturally rely on functional idioms for the power and tendency toward simplification that they provide. If you read this book carefully, study the examples, and start to incorporate some functional ideas into your code, you will soon see great benefits.

 You may even decide you want to investigate some programming languages that provide more support for the functional paradigm. Languages such as Scala, Clojure, F#, and Haskell, to name a few.

Scala

A note about the examples in this book. I will be providing examples in various languages. This is to demonstrate the way different languages implement functional ideas. While it is possible to write functional code in various languages (with varying levels of ease depending on the language), some languages make it a lot easier to do and are generally more powerful because of this. One such language is Scala.

There are two things I want to say about Scala:

- Scala is a concise language
- Scala is conducive to writing functional code

So while we will be including examples in Java, Python, and C#, most of the examples will be in Scala. For a short introduction to Scala, see the Appendix. Especially when describing category theory, Scala is a good choice. I would argue that a language like Scala allows for more concise functional constructs and in many cases it may drive a point home to show how to do it in Scala. There are other languages I could have used for this purpose—other languages that are functional to one degree or another—Haskell (which is exceedingly functional), Clojure, and Meta Language (ML) for example. I simply felt that the clarity of Scala and the ease with which one can write functional code made it a good choice for many of the examples in this book.

If you have been using Java and you are interested in FP, you may want to try out Scala. I would argue that, especially for greenfield projects, you might find it useful, productive, and fun.

I mentioned that this book will contain examples in Scala, Java, Python, and C#. But as we get deeper into function concepts, it will be more useful to craft our examples in Scala. Especially when we learn about some of the abstract concepts in FP. There are different degrees of FP. Some languages are partly functional and others are fully or *purely* functional, as we say.

In Table 1-1, you'll see a chart comparing the languages used in examples throughout the book. I have also included Haskell, even though I don't use Haskell examples, because it is an example of a purely functional programming language and it is good as a means of comparison.

Table 1-1. Support for functional versus object-oriented programming in several languages

	Scala	Java	Python	C#	Haskell[a]
Supports functional	YES	PARTLY	PARTLY	PARTLY	YES
Supports purely functional	NO	NO	NO	NO	YES
Supports OOP	YES	YES	YES	YES	PARTLY

[a] Haskell was created to be a purely functional language. For example, once you set the value of a variable, you cannot change it. It has many other functional features, many of which come from category theory. We will see category theory in Chapter 3.

Conclusion

In this chapter we have looked broadly at the major features that make up an FP language. As the book progresses, we will get deeper into these features and how the fundamental patterns of FP are reflected in them.

CHAPTER 2

Mathematical Preliminaries

This chapter presents some material that you will need to know (and may well have learned at some point in the past). It will mostly cover basic facts about functions both from a mathematical and a computer science point of view. Feel free to skip this chapter and move on to Chapter 3 if you don't need a mathematical refresher.

Set Theory

Set theory is a huge field. For our purposes, we just need a few basic definitions from set theory. You would think that set theory provides a definition of *set*. Actually, *set* is taken as an undefined term in set theory and we informally think of it as a collection of objects. We can talk about the set of even numbers, the set that consists of 0, 1, and 2, the set that contains my mother and my father; anything we can conceive of as a collection is a set.[1] We generally denote sets by capital letters A, B, C, etc. We call the things *in* a set, *elements*. If every element of A is also an element of B, we say that A is a subset of B or A is contained in B, as you'll see in Figure 2-1.

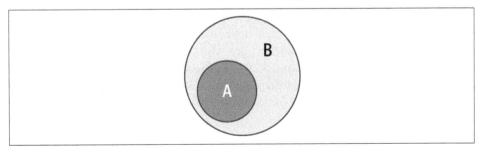

Figure 2-1. A is a subset of B

---

1 Set theorists do distinguish between a set and a class, but we will not worry about this distinction in this book.

The intersection of two sets is the set that contains all the elements that are in both A and B, as you will see in Figure 2-2.

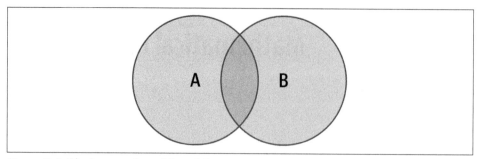

Figure 2-2. The intersection of A and B

The union of A and B is the set that consists of all the elements that are in A or B. See Figure 2-3.

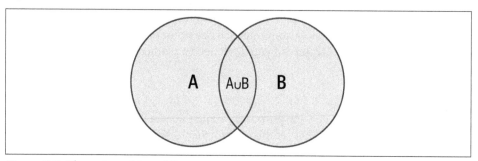

Figure 2-3. The union of A and B

Functions

In plain language, a function is a rule that associates every element in one set with some element in another set. The idea here is that we have a bunch of things and we associate each one with something in a second bunch of things. A simple example from mathematics is the square function defined on all whole numbers. This function maps each whole number to its square: 1 goes to 1, 2 goes to 4, 3 goes to 9, etc. Also, –1 goes to 1, –2 goes to 4, and so on. So we see that a function can take two different values to the same value. The opposite is not true. One element cannot be mapped to two different elements. The things functions are defined on are sets.

Domain and range

A function is defined on a bunch of elements. The more mathematical term for this is a set of elements. The set of all elements that the function is defined on is called the *domain* of the function. An important point here is that if we have a formula defining a function, for example, the square function, we can pick all positive whole numbers as the domain and we can also pick all whole numbers, positive and negative, to be the domain. These are considered two different functions even though both are defined by the square function. Therefore, whenever we define a function, we should specify the domain.

The *range* of a function is the set of all elements that get mapped to by some element in the domain. In the example of the square function with domain equal to all whole numbers, the range would be all the whole numbers that are the square of some whole number. In this case, the range is all positive integers because the square of a whole number is always either 0 or a positive whole number.

So every function has a domain and a range. We specify the domain and then the range is determined by what the function does to elements in the domain. Sometimes we will see the following:

```
f: A -> B
```

The author may say something like, "Let f be a function from A to B." The author might say explicitly, "f is a function with domain A and range B." In this case, of course, we know the range is B. Sometimes, however, the author will say, "Let f be a function from A to B." In this case, it might be that the range is a *subset* of B. In other words, every element of A gets mapped to an element of B but *not* every element of B is "hit" by some element in A. In this case, A is the domain and B *contains* the range. In this case, B is called the *codomain*.

So when we see:

```
f: A -> B
```

We know the range is a subset (possibly the whole thing) of B, as you'll see in Figure 2-4.

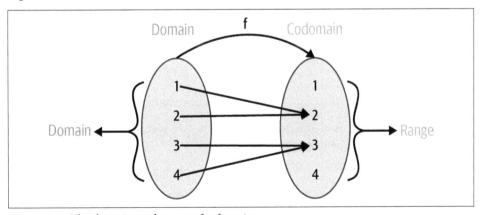

Figure 2-4. The domain and range of a function

Example 2-1 illustrates domain and range.

Example 2-1. Domain and range of a function

Let's define f to be the absolute value function with domain equal to all whole numbers. We take a number like –3, and map it to its absolute value, 3. Let's say we see this written as:

```
abs: Z -> Z
```

Here Z denotes the set of whole numbers. (This comes from the German word for whole number, Zahlen.) The key point here is that while the absolute value of any whole number is either 0 or is positive, it is not the case that every whole number is the absolute value of some number. For example, no whole number has an absolute value of -3. The domain of this function is Z, while all whole numbers and the codomain of this function is also Z. The *range*, on the other hand, is N, the natural numbers. The natural numberes are all positive whole numbers together with 0.

 Be careful to distinguish between the range and the codomain of a function.

Kinds of Functions

I pointed out previously that while two different elements in the domain can be mapped to the same element in the range, the opposite cannot happen. We can't have one element in the domain being mapped to two distinct elements of the range. This is because if somebody asked you what x is mapped to, you need to be able to offer a single, correct answer so that an element of the domain gets mapped to one and only one element in the range. What about the case where two different elements in the domain get mapped to the same element in the range? This can happen. If we have a function where this *doesn't* happen, we have a name for this function, discussed in the next section.

One-to-one functions

A one-to-one function is a function in which no two elements in the domain, get mapped to the same element in the range.

Consider the function `f: Z -> Z` defined by `f(n) = 2 * n`.

This function takes a whole number and returns two times that number. I claim that f is one-to-one. We can demonstrate this by assuming a and b are both mapped to c, then we show that *a* is actually equal to *b*. This will show that two different elements can't be mapped to the same element.

Suppose:

```
f(a) = f(b)
```

This means:

```
2 * a = 2 * b
```

Now we divide both sides by 2 and we get:

```
a = b
```

This proves *f* is one-to-one. Next, let's look at a function that is not one-to-one. For the following equation, the domain is all whole numbers:

```
f(n) = n * n
```

All we have to do is show that there are two different whole numbers that both get mapped to the same number, e.g. 3 and –3. If we square these numbers, we get 9 for both of them. Therefore *f* is *not* one-to-one. (It is, of course, a perfectly good function, just not one-to-one.)

Onto functions

A function is *onto* if its codomain is equal to its range. Another way of saying this is: Let *f* be a function from *A* to *B*. If for every element *b* in *B*, there is an element *a* in *A* when *f*(*a*) = *b*, then *f* is *onto*.

Let *f* be a function from *N* to *N* with *f*(*m*) = *m* × *m*.

If this is onto, then for any *n* in *N*, there is an *m* in *N* with *m* × *m* = *n*. This would be saying that every natural number is a perfect square, which we know is not true. For example, 5 is a natural number. Which natural number has 5 as its square? None of them. So *f* is *not* onto.

Now let's consider another function. Let *f* be a function from *N* to *N* defined by *f*(*n*) = |*n*|, the absolute value of *n*. If I take any natural number, can I find another natural number whose absolute value is equal to the given natural number? Well, what about 3? Then *f*(3) = |3| = 3, so that works. In fact, since any natural number is not negative, it is *equal* to its own absolute value. So this function *is* onto.

You may see these ideas expressed using different vocabulary. Another term for one-to-one is *injective*. And another term for onto is *surjective*.

Computer Science Fundamentals

In this section we will discuss a few, mostly unrelated concepts that are relevant to programming in general.

Anonymous Functions

The usual way of defining a function in a programming language is to use keywords (such as *def*, *function*, or *sub*), give the function a name, and then fill in the body of the function. You can then call that function by its name. In Scala, we can define a function that squares an integer as follows:

```
def square(n: Int): Int = n * n
```

Then, you can call it like this:

```
println(square(3))  //prints 9 to the console.
```

This approach lets us define a function once and use it as many times as we need. However, there may be times when we need to call a function only once, and many programming languages facilitate this. These are generally called anonymous functions. Here is how we write the square function as an anonymous function in Scala:

```
(n: Int) => n * n
```

How might we use this? Suppose we want to define a function *f* that takes another function as its argument and applies that other function to 3. Undoubtedly, this is somewhat contrived, but it makes the point. In Scala, we could do this:

```
def f(g: Int => Int): Int = g(3)
```

Then we could call *f* on the square function like this:

```
f((n: Int) => n*n)
```

We can do this without ever defining the square function.

For historical reasons, anonymous functions are sometimes called *lambda* functions.[2] Some languages, notably Python, use `lambda` as a keyword, when constructing anonymous functions. Here is `square` in Python:

```
def square(n):
    return n * n
```

Here it is as an anonymous function:

```
lambda n: n * n
```

---

2 This refers to the lambda calculus, arguably the first programming language.

Functions as First Class Objects

FP languages make it easy to treat functions as first class objects. This means that anything you can do with any other object or variable, you can do with functions. For example, if *f* is a first class object, you can pass it as a parameter to another function and you can return it from a function as a return value. Here are some examples in Scala:

```
def call(n: Int, f: Int=>Int): Int  = f(n)
```

The `call` function takes an `Int` and a function for an `Int` to an `Int` and applies the function to the `Int`.

```
def addN(n: Int): Int => Int = (m: Int) => m+n

val f = addN(3)

println(f(5))  //returns 8 s
```

The `addN` function takes an integer `n` and returns a function that takes an integer `m`, adding `n` to it.

Conclusion

Hopefully you have a good sense now of some of the basic properties of functions.[3] In the next chapter, we'll dive into category theory and patterns, and you'll see how these topics are used.

---

3 But see the Appendix for a fuller treatment of functions, in the context of Scala.

CHAPTER 3

Category Theory and Patterns

In this chapter, I will introduce software patterns and describe how they work in FP. I will also introduce category theory and explain how it can be useful as a source of functional software patterns and also how it is the foundation from which FP comes.

A software pattern (*https://oreil.ly/TILR8*) is a reusable solution to a commonly occurring problem within a given context in software design. Software patterns mean that we do not have to start from scratch every time we write code. A software pattern is a template for solving a type of problem. The more of these templates you know about, the better equipped you are to tackle a given development obstacle. Once these patterns become second nature and you no longer have to look them up, you will become a more proficient developer.

 A pattern is just a tool for helping you formulate your code. Most of the problems we attempt to solve in software creation have already been solved in a universal, efficient manner. A pattern describes one of these solutions.

Patterns were popularized by the Gang of Four software patterns book (*https://oreil.ly/kH7VD*). This book put patterns on the map and they have since become a popular tool for programmers to use. Now, if you ask functional programmers about patterns, they may say that patterns are not particularly relevant in FP. When they say this, they are likely thinking of the traditional, OOP patterns found in the Gang of Four book. However, there is another set of structures commonly used by functional programmers that they simply may not think of as patterns. These structures come from a branch of mathematics called category theory. I choose to call these *functional patterns* and will investigate them next.

Let us call patterns that come from category theory "functional patterns" to distinguish them from the patterns that come from the Gang of Four book.

Let us consider an example. The example we will consider has to do with the `null` keyword. It is well known that there are problems associated with the `null` keyword and one of the biggest is the `NullPointerException`. There is a functional pattern called the Option pattern. Let's say you are a Scala programmer and you are writing some code with a `null` in it. Let's say you have something like this:

Scala

```scala
case class User(name: String)

def getUser(uid: Int): User = {
    return getUserFromDB(uid)
}
```

Let us suppose `getUserFromDB` returns a `null` if it doesn't find a user for the given `uid`. Now, there is a risk of you calling `user.name`. If `user` is `null`, this will throw a `NullPointerException` and your program may crash, depending on whether you handle the `NullPointerException` or not. Letting your code throw `NullPointer Exceptions` is risky.

 Beware of `NullPointerExceptions` in your code. The best way to avoid them is to never have a function return a `null`. The functional pattern Option is a good way to avoid `NullPointer Exceptions`.

Now let's say you know about the functional pattern *Option*. The Option pattern is perfect for problems that involve a `null` value. The idea is to have an object represent the case that nulls are used for but to do it with a type. The `Option` trait addresses this problem exactly. `Option` comes in two flavors. `Some()`, a wrapper around a value, such as `Some(user)`, and `None`, which represents the case where there is no answer, the case often expressed by `null`. But `None` has a type and so the compiler can check that the code is correct. `NullPointerExceptions` are something that happen at run time, not compile time, and use of the Option pattern helps to avoid this situation. Let us rewrite the earlier `getUser` method with `Option`. The following example shows how `Options` can be processed with pattern matching.

The Option class comes in two flavors: Some and None. Some wraps another value, like Some(user), and None means that no value was found. You can unwrap an Option with pattern matching.

Scala

```scala
case class User(name: String)
def getUser(uid: Int): Option[User] = {
    getUserFromDB(uid) match {
        case Some(user) => //do something with user
        case None => //no user was found
    }
}
```

This code is checkable at compile time and there is no possibility of a NullPointer Exception. Option is a software pattern and is what I would call a functional pattern. For more on Options, see "The Option Type" on page 112.

Category Theory–Based Patterns

It is not absolutely critical that you know about category theory to be a good functional programmer. It *will* help, but if you prefer to learn more by code examples, you can skip the material on category theory. Later in the book, we will investigate functional patterns by means of code examples.

I like to think of these patterns as hardcore FP patterns. Functional programmers who lean towards pure FP use these idioms liberally in their code. Along with immutability, referential transparency, and higher order functions, these patterns form the main content of what it means for code to be functional.

Functional programs use code constructs that are immutable, obey referential transparency, use higher order functions, and make liberal use of functional patterns.

The Functor, Monoid, and Monad patterns are some examples of category theory–based patterns. Before we dive into their details, though, I'd like to present a brief history of category theory as a discipline of mathematics. Who knows, you might just find you like category theory as a subject in its own right.

Category theory is a branch of mathematics initially concerned with finding similar constructs within different areas of mathematics. It is a unifying theory. It later was applied to FP.

A Brief History

In the 1940s, Saunders Mac Lane and Samuel Eilenberg were discussing a lecture one of them gave. They both came to the same conclusion, together, that the subjects each was working on, one in algebra and one in topology, were actually instances of the same phenomenon. After fleshing out their ideas, they realized they had discovered a new subject. Thus was born category theory! So while category theory is a distinct branch of mathematics from algebra and topology, its roots lie in these two subjects. The fundamental concepts of FP come from category theory. With a solid understanding of the basic concepts of category theory, these concepts will be easier to understand and adapt in the context of FP. Learning some category theory is like learning FP from a totally different perspective. And each new perspective makes your understanding deeper.

Learning some category theory can substantially deepen your understanding of FP. It can also give you ideas about new FP constructs.

Mac Lane and Eilenberg cowrote a book entitled *Categories for the Working Mathematician*, which became a big source for future development in the subject. Then, in 1990, the purely FP language Haskell was created. Many ideas were taken from category theory in creating Haskell. Some of these concepts have found their way into other functional and partly FP languages, such as Scala, F#, and Java, to name a few. Another way functional capabilities were incorporated into programming practice was through software libraries.

Objects and Morphisms

The basic definition of category theory involves two concepts, objects and morphisms.

Objects in category theory have nothing to do with objects in OOP. They are totally unrelated concepts.

In category theory, *objects* can be anything: sets, numbers, matrices, just to name a few. In addition to having objects, a category also needs something called morphisms. A *morphism* can be defined only in the context of two objects from the category. Let us suppose that A and B are objects from a category C. Then a morphism is an arrow from A to B.

We write it like this:

$$A \rightarrow B$$

But what does an arrow mean, exactly? Well, it connects object A to object B. Where the arrow starts and where the arrow ends is the information that defines the morphism.

A morphism from object A to object B is an arrow from A to B. You could also think of it as a pair of objects in a particular order.

People tend to think of this arrow as a function, in part because the earlier expression makes it look like a function, and in most cases it *is* a function. There are categories where the morphisms are not functions—but they are rare, so for our purposes, morphisms will always be functions. Think of it this way: objects are sets and morphisms are functions from one set to another.

While it is theoretically possible to have morphisms that are not functions, for our purposes, objects will always be sets and morphisms will be functions between the sets.

Now if f is a morphism from A to B, then A is called the domain of f and B is called the codomain of f. This corresponds to the language used for functions. See "Functions" on page 104 for more details.

An Example of a Category

Let us start with the category of all sets. That is, the objects are all sets.

A set is just a collection of objects. The objects can be numbers, people, or even other sets. We are about to consider the category whose objects are *all* sets.

We consider the category called Set. The objects are all sets. What are the morphisms? Simply all functions from A to B. Every function from A to B is a morphism. So the category Set is the category whose objects are sets and morphisms are functions from A to B, for all pairs of sets, A and B. A is called the domain of the morphism and B is called the codomain of the morphism. For review, see "Functions" on page 104.

Now, let's look more deeply into the category Set. The following example shows two objects, *A* and *B* in the category Set and two morphisms with domain *A* and codomain *B*.

Let $A = \{1,2,3,4\}$ and $B = \{a,b,c,d,e\}$.

These are two perfectly good sets so they are objects in the category Set. Let us now define two morphisms from *A* to *B*.

Morphism f from A to B
> For all *x* in *A*, $f(x) = a$. This could be called a constant morphism. This is just the function that takes every element of *A* to the element *a* of the set *B*.

Morphism g from A to B
> $g(1) = a$
>
> $g(2) = b$
>
> $g(3) = c$
>
> $g(4) = d$

The two functions from *A* to *B* are two morphisms in the category Set. Note that this is a very large category. It contains *all* sets and *all* functions from *A* to *B*.

Before we look at some more examples, there are a couple of things about morphisms we have to say. First, morphisms compose. What does this mean? We will give the actual definition of two morphisms composing, but the general idea is that when you compose two morphisms, you call one morphism and then apply the second morphism to the result of calling the first morphism.

For example, suppose $f: A \rightarrow B$ is a morphism, and $g: B \rightarrow C$ is a morphism. Since we are in a category, there must exist a morphism *h* from *A* to *C* satisfying:

$$h(x) = g(f(x))$$

 $g(f(x))$ means first evaluate $f(x)$ and then apply *g* to it.

We denote *h* by the expression *g* o *f* and we say this as *f composed with g*.

If *f* is a morphism from *A* to *B*, and *g* is a morphism from *B* to *C*, then there must exist a morphism *h* from *A* to *C* where for all *x* in *A*, $h(x) = g(f(x))$. In this case, we denote *h* with the expression *g* o *f* and call it *f composed with g*.

If the composition *h* does not exist, then what we were considering was not a category. In *every* category, morphisms must compose.

There is one other property morphisms must have in order to have a category: for each object *A* in the category, there must exist a morphism id_A: *A* → *A* with the property that for any morphism *f*: *A* → *B* and morphism *g*: *A* → *B* in the category, we have:

$$f \text{ o } id_A = f$$

and

$$id_B \text{ o } g = g$$

This is just the category theory way of saying that id_A is the identity function on *A*. The identity function on *A* is just the function that takes every element of *A* to itself.

 The identity function on a set A is the function that maps every element to itself. The category theory version of this is that the identity morphism on A, denoted id_A, when it composes with another function, leaves that function unchanged.

Category theorists tend to think not in terms of points, but rather in terms of composition of functions. The earlier expression is how you express the identity function in category theory in terms of composition. Instead of saying identity morphism takes every point in the object to itself (because we don't think about the points), you say that when you compose the identity morphism with another morphism, you get the original morphism back.

 Much of category theory is about expressing structure through the notion of composition. Where does this show up in FP? It shows up when we compose functions.

Let's look at an example of composing the `length` function. `length` takes a string and returns an integer denoting the length of that string. `square` is a function that takes an integer and returns an integer denoting the square of the given integer. Let's compose the two.

Scala

```
(square o length)("abc") == square(length("abc")) == square(3) = 9
```

In this example, we composed `length` with `square` and got another morphism, denoted `square o length`.

Let's look at some more examples of categories. We will need something called a semigroup. A *semigroup* has two main parts, a set of elements, (could be any non-empty set) and a binary operation on the set. A binary operation, like multiplication for whole numbers, takes two things and returns a third thing. There is one condition that must hold. The binary operation must be associative. We will denote the binary operation with an asterisk (*).

Something is associative when for all x, y, and z, we have: x * (y * z) = (x * y) * z

A semigroup is a non-empty set with an associative binary operation on it.

As an example, let the set be all whole numbers and let the operation be multiplication. First, notice that when we multiply two numbers together, we get another whole number. This is necessary for a semigroup. When you combine two elements in a semigroup with the binary operation, you should get something that is again in the semigroup.[1] We won't prove it here, but multiplication on whole numbers is associative. So all whole numbers multiplied by each other form a semigroup.

Here is another example. Let the set be all 3 × 3 matrices of real numbers. If you don't know what a matrix is, feel free to skip this example. The operation will be multiplication of matrices. One can show this is associative. It just so happens that matrix multiplication is not commutative. A * B is not necessarily equal to B * A. However, commutativity is not a requirement for something to be a semigroup; associativity is necessary.

I've shown you two examples of semigroups, but suppose we want to study *all* semigroups at once. In this case, we could study the *category* of semigroups. What are the morphisms? This is a bit more involved. We might want to say that the morphisms are functions from one semigroup to another semigroup, but this would not be sufficient. Category theory is all about structure and finding similar structures in seemingly different objects, so what structure does a semigroup have? The structure is determined by the multiplication operation.

---

1 For example, negative numbers with multiplication couldn't form a semigroup because when you multiply two negative numbers, you don't get another negative number.

In a semigroup, we often call the binary operation multiplication, even if it is not necessarily the usual multiplication of numbers.

The notion of morphism, in this case, has to somehow capture the multiplicative structure of the semigroup. In the following example, I'll show you how this works.

Let S_1 and S_2 be two objects in the category Semigroup.

A function h from S_1 to S_2 is a morphism if for all x, y in S_1, we have:

$$h(x * y) = h(x) * h(y)$$

This means that the two semigroups have similar multiplicative structure. It says if you want to know where h maps $x * y$, just look at where h maps x and where h maps y and then multiply them together in S_2. You can think of the morphism as renaming the object it maps. In this case, x in S_1 corresponds to $h(x)$ in S_2. And y in S_1 corresponds to $h(y)$ in S_2. h being a morphism means that $x * y$ corresponds to $h(x) * h(y)$. It is like an alternate universe in which every entity in the original universe has a corresponding partner in the alternate universe.

What does all of this have to do with FP? In the next section, I'll explain.

The Category Scal

When it comes down to it, even though much of FP theory comes to us from category theory, often through the programming language Haskell, we are really interested in only one particular category.

First, select a programming language. In theory, it can be any programming language with types. We will choose Scala, because it is particularly suited to functional constructions and because much of Scala code is sufficiently clear that it almost resembles pseudocode. I call this category *Scal*, because of the well-established category Hask, associated with the Haskell language.

The objects in the category Scal are the set of all types of Scala—not only simple types like String, Int, and Boolean, but also List[String], Map[Int,Double], and any type we can build up from basic ones. We could also include user-defined types like User, Account, etc. In theory, we could look at the category for any programming language with types. We are working with the category Scal, but if we wanted to, we could work with a category based on, say, Java. In this case, the objects would be types in the Java language.

The objects in the category Scal are all the types of Scala. `String`, `List[Int]`, and `Map[Int,User]` are all objects in the category Scal.

Morphisms

If we take two types, say `String` and `Int`, how should we define a morphism between them? Simply define a morphism from `String` to `Int` as any function that takes a `String` and returns an `Int`. An example of a morphism between these two types would be the length function. It takes a `String` (e.g., "abc") and returns an `Int`, in this case, 3.

If A and B are types in Scala, a morphism from A to B is a function that takes an A and returns a B.

Consider the following example of the composition of two morphisms. We know that in any category, if there is a morphism $f\colon A \to B$ and a morphism $g\colon B \to C$, then there must be a morphism $h\colon A \to C$ with $h = g \circ f$. Let's take two morphisms that line up the right way and see what their composition is.

$f\colon$ `String` $\to$ `Int` is defined by $f(s) =$ `s.length`
$g\colon$ `Int` $\to$ `Int` is defined by $g(n) = n * n$

So f is the `length` function and g is the `square` function. What does their composition look like? $(g \circ f)(s) =$ `s.length * s.length`

We have our category Scal where the objects are types and for two types, A and B, the morphisms are functions that take an A and return a B.

Once you have selected a programming language—Scala, in this case—all the category theory that is applied to FP deals with this one category Scal, where the objects are Scala's types and the morphisms from A to B are functions that take an object of type A and return an object of type B.

Functors

Functor is a funny word. It sounds like function and it is, indeed, a function. But it is a special kind of function. Before we define it, let's look at some examples in Scala that correspond to functors. Some functors in Scala are List, Option, and Future.[2] These examples have two things in common. First, they are generic types, meaning that they take other types as parameters. You can't just have a List in Scala. You *can* have List[String], List[Int], or List[User], though (among others). List[String] is not a functor. It is a type. List by itself is a functor.

List[String] is not a functor. It is a type. List by itself is a functor. When you apply it to a type, like String, for example, you get a type. This is why, in Scala, a functor is also called a type constructor.

Another consideration is that all functors have a map function. Let's see an example.

Scala

```
val lst = List(1,2,3,4)  ❶
lst.map(n => n*n)         ❷
//returns List(1,4,9,16)
```

❶   Create a list of four numbers.

❷   List is a functor so it has a map function.

Now, let's define "functor." I first need to specify two categories: C_1 and C_2.

Then a functor F from C_1 to C_2 is a function from the first category to the second category, which satisfies the following properties.

1. F takes objects in C_1 to objects in C_2. (Just like List takes String to List[String].)

2. F takes morphisms in C_1 to morphisms in C_2. (What List does to a morphism is trickier. It involves the map function and we will address this next.)

3. $F(f \circ g) = F(f) \circ F(g)$ whenever the morphism domains and codomains of f and g line up.

This condition basically means that the two categories C_1 and C_2 have similar structure with respect to morphisms. The idea to keep in mind when considering functors is that they measure how similar two categories are.

---

2 For more coverage of these concepts, see the Appendix.

To define a functor, we first need two categories, C_1 and C_2. Then, a functor is a function from C_1 to C_2 that satisfies certain properties we describe next.

Don't we need two categories to define a functor? No. A functor can go from a category to itself. Such a functor is called an *endofunctor*. All of the functors we will be considering, in the category Scal, will be endofunctors.

Let's consider the List type constructor in Scala. (Notice it isn't a *type*). A List has to be a List of something. List by itself is not a type. List[String], for example, is a type. On the other hand, a List by itself is a type constructor. It "constructs" a type because when you take a List of something, you get a type. What are some other examples like this in Scala? Option and Future, to name a few.

In the category Scal, these are examples of functors: List, Option, and Future. They are functors from the category Scal to itself.

Remember, we called such a functor an endofunctor. List, Option, and Future are examples of endofunctors, and all endofunctors are functors.

What does a functor do to a morphism?

First, List takes objects of Scal to objects of Scal. For example, List takes the object String to the object List[String]. Second, List also takes morphisms to morphisms. How does this work? Let us consider the two morphisms length and square. length is a morphism from String to Int and square is a morphism from Int to Int. Their composition square o length is a morphism from String to Int. It takes a string and spits out the square of the string's length.[3]

So, we understand how List takes String to List[String], but how does List act on the morphisms? What is List(length)? This looks odd. We are not accustomed to taking the list of a function.[4] What can this mean? Since length goes from String to Int, List(length) must go from List[String] to List[Int]. Can you think of any function, possibly with another name, that maps List[String] to List[Int]? If you thought of map, you are correct. In Scala, we would write this:

---

3 This is a bit contrived, I know, but it illustrates composition of morphisms.

4 Unless it's a list of functions. In this example, we do not mean a list of functions. We are applying List to the function as a functor.

Scala

```
List("abc", "defgh").map(_.length) //== List(3,5)
```

In Scala, certain types have a map function defined. (We will see that these are precisely the functors.) Therefore, given a functor, there is this map function in the background. When we want to know what the functor does to a morphism, we need to use the map function in a certain way. We expressed this earlier with length, but let us see what this looks like in a more general case.

 Functors turn up in FP anywhere there are types that implement the map function. Think functor = mappable trait (or interface).

Let's look at an example in the category Scal.

Consider the functor List from Scala to Scala. We said that a functor maps objects to objects and morphisms to morphisms. In this case, List is taking an object A in Scal to the object List[A] in Scala. Remember, objects in Scal are types.

What about what the functor List does to morphisms? Let A = String and B = Int and let's see what List does to length: $A \rightarrow B$.

Well, List(length) has to be a morphism in Scal. And since length goes from String to Int, we know that List(length) goes from List[String] to List[Int]. Let's take an object of type List[String] and see what List(length) does to it.

```
List(length)(List("abc")) = List("abc").map(s => s.length)
```

The preceding equation is equal to List(3).

In Scala, we don't think of this function as List(length), but rather as the map function. There are actually many map functions, one for each functor. In Scala, we think of this as just one map function, which can be applied to any container-like data structure. In category theory, the map function is what you get when you apply a functor to a morphism.

I mentioned earlier that you could skip our theoretical treatment of category theory in FP. I said that we would look at it in a purely practical way. This is what we will do next for functors.

Programming Language Formulation of a Functor

What is a functor in programming language terms? A functor is simply an interface (or trait in Scala) that implements the map method.

A functor could have been called Mappable because it is simply a trait with a `map` method defined. When you see *functor*, think *has a map method*.

As we have seen, there are two ways of looking at a functor. We can represent functor as a trait (or interface) that implements the `map` method or we can think of it the way we think of it in category theory. From this perspective, a functor is a function from the types of Scala to the types of Scala and it is also a function from morphisms in the category Scal to other morphisms in Scal. In particular, if A and B are two Scala types, and f is a morphism from A to B, then F(f) is a morphism from F[A] to F[B]. We could think of F as providing a context for two types and a morphism between them. We start off working in A and in B and end up working in F[A] and F[B]. So we have contextualized A and B. If I want to know what represents the morphism f in the context F, we look at the morphism F(f) from F[A] to F[B]. What is this morphism? Well, if fa is an element of F[A], then F(f) takes fa to fa.map(f).

Remember, every functor has a `map` method associated with it, so we can always carry out the expression. Let me give an example. I can use the functor `List`. In this example, A = Int and B = Int. F = List and let the morphism square f: A -> B be the `square` function.

Then F[A] = List[Int] and F[B] = List[Int], too. What is F(square)? That is to say, what is List(square)? Remember, for this we need the `map` function that comes along with List (as it does with every functor). We write all of this as follows:

```
F(square)(fa) = fa.map(f) or
List(square)(fa) = fa.map(square)
```

This gives us:

```
List(square)(List(1,2,3,4)) = List(1,2,3,4).map(square) = List(1,4,9,16)
```

We know that there are three properties a functor from category C to category D must satisfy:

- A functor F takes objects in C to objects in D. In the case of the category Scal, this means F takes Scala types to Scala types.
- F takes morphisms in C to morphisms in D.
- A composition property, seen here:

  $F(f \circ g) = F(f) \circ F(g)\$$ where f and g are morphisms.

Let us check this property for the functor List and two morphisms length and square.[5] Here, length is a morphism from String to Int and square is a morphism from Int to Int.

Plugging in the values, I have to prove the following:

```
List(square o length) = List(square) o List(length)
```

Now the expression on the left takes an object of type List[String] to an object of type List[Int]. For example:

```
List(square o length)(List("hello", "universe")) =
List("hello","universe").map(square o length) =
List(square o length ("hello"), square o length ("universe")) =
List(square(5), square(8)) = List(25,64)
```

Now let's evaluate List(square) o List(length).

```
List(square) o List(length))(List("hello","universe")) =
List(square)(List(length)(List("hello","universe"))) =
List(square)(List("hello","universe").map(length) =
List(square)(List(5,8) = List(5,8).map(square) = List(25,64)
```

The two sides are equal. What we have shown, in this particular case, is in fact always true. For any functor F and two morphisms f and g, we always have:

$$F(f \circ g) = F(f) \circ F(g)$$

All of these calculations show that F does satisfy this important property of a functor, namely $F(f \circ g) = F(f) \circ F(g)$.

This will hold for other functors, such as Option and Future. Once we know something is a functor, we know we can compose morphisms in this way. Why do we care? In the next section, I'll explain.

The Patterns

In this section, we describe some functional patterns. These patterns occur frequently in functional code and being familiar with them is certain to assist you in writing functional code in the future. We start with the most common functional pattern, the Functor pattern.

---

5 This part is a bit formula heavy. Feel free to skip it if it's not your thing.

The Functor Pattern

We now have some idea of what a functor is, but how are they useful? Functors are useful for two reasons:

- They always have a map function.
- They can always be composed.

In the following example, I will show you how composing two functors can be useful.

Suppose we have a list of options:

Scala

```
val listOfOptions = List(Some(8), None, Some(2))
```

If you are unfamiliar with `Some` and `None`, see "The Option Type" on page 112. Suppose we want to add up the numbers 1, 8, and 2. Most languages don't provide functor constructions out of the box. Even Scala, which is fairly functional, doesn't have this capability. There is a library called Cats (*https://oreil.ly/lXxBp*), however, which provides category theory constructs as "first class" objects.

 In the functional Scala community, Cats is the go-to library for functional constructs.

First, let's look at the trait `Functor`, which comes with Cats.

Scala

```
trait Functor[F[_]] {
    def map[A, B](fa: F[A])(f: A => B): F[B]
}
```

We can see the `map` function, which every functor has. But what is `F[_]`? `F[_]` is Scala's way of expressing a type constructor. So the `F`, here, is what we are thinking of as the functor. Remember, we want to illustrate how composition of functors, which you always have, is useful. Back to our example of `listOfOptions`:

```
val listOfOptions = List(Some(8), None, Some(2))
```

The definition of the trait `Functor` in the Scala library Cats is much simplified for our example. One method it comes with is `compose`. To add 1 to the numbers in the options, we can do the following:

Scala

```
Functor[List].compose[Option].map(listOption)(_ + 1)
```

We have a list of options of `Ints` and we want to `map` over the `Ints`. This expression lets us compose `List` and `Option` to get a new functor, and then use that new functor's `map` method to map over the `Ints` with the anonymous function `_ + 1`, which is just Scala's way of writing an anonymous function that adds 1. We started with:

```
val listOfOptions = List(Some(8), None, Some(2))
```

and ended up with:

```
val listOfOptions = List(Some(9), None, Some(3))
```

Notice that a lot of meaning is packed into this expression. This is a good example of the power of composition of functors for FP.

Monoids

As I mentioned earlier in the chapter, a semigroup is a set with an associative operation on it. If a semigroup has an identify element, which means an element e in the semigroup with the property that: $e * x = x * e = x$ for all elements x in the semigroup, the semigroup is called a *monoid*.

In Examples 3-1 and 3-2, I'll show you some examples of monoids.

Example 3-1. Example of a monoid

Let M be the set of all nonnegative whole numbers. Along with the operation addition, this is a semigroup. But notice that 0 is in the set M. We know that if we add 0 to any nonnegative whole number on the left or right, you get the original whole number back.

 We say left side or right side because not all semigroups are commutative. It's not always true, in a semigroup, that $a * b = b * a$.

In the case of nonnegative whole numbers, addition is commutative. So saying left side and right side in the definition is unnecessary. This is a monoid. We can write it like this: `(N, + , 0)`.

Example 3-2. Another example of a monoid

Let M be the set of all 2×2 integer matrices with matrix multiplication. With the identity matrix, the one with ones on the diagonal and zeros off the diagonal, this is a monoid. Note that matrix multiplication is not commutative in general, but if you multiply the identity matrix on the left or right of a given matrix, you get that matrix back again.

How are monoids useful in FP?

Let us start with a simple example. We want a function that adds up a bunch of numbers. Let's write this code in Java in a common, imperative style. We might do something obvious, such as the following:

Java

```java
int sum(List<Integer> lst) {
        int result = 0;
        for (int i=0; i<lst.size(); i++) {
            result += lst.get(i);
        }
        return result;
    }
```

This code computes the sum of a list of integers. Let's analyze it from a functional perspective. First, notice how it mutates state. The value of result continually changes throughout the program. So does the value of i. Let us try to write a functional version of this function that does not mutate state, which also uses monoid to express the sum with a higher level of abstraction. There is a function in FP called foldLeft.[6] Essentially, foldLeft comes out of the concept of a monoid. If you have a monoid, you can implement foldLeft.

Let's see an example. Consider the following monoid: the set of integers with addition as the operation and 0 as the identity element. We can create the foldLeft function in any monoid. We combine the identity with the first element of the monoid. Then we take the result of that and combine it on the left with the next element in the monoid. We do this until there are no more elements. Another way of saying this is that we are given a binary operation, that is, one that combines two elements. And fold applies the operation pairwise to get the combination of all the elements. In Java, there is a similar function called reduce. Let's see an example:

Java

```java
Integer sumAll(List<Integer>lst) {
        return lst.stream().reduce(0, Integer::sum);
    }
```

---

6 There is also a foldRight. You will see this function with various names depending on the programming language—e.g., foldLeft, foldl, foldRight, foldr, and fold.

In Scala, we have:

Scala

```scala
def sumAll(Lst: List[Integer]):
    return lst.foldLeft(0)(_+_)
```

In Scala, `foldLeft` is a method in the `List[Int]` class and `_ + _` is an anonymous function. `foldLeft` can be used in many situations. For every monoid in a category, there is a `foldLeft` function. For example, strings with concatenation or booleans with `and`. No matter how complex monoids get, there is always a `foldLeft` function you can use. This illustrates how we can get a useful function, `foldLeft`, that comes directly from the categorical notion of a monoid. `foldLeft` is a vast generalization of adding up a bunch of numbers, concatenating a bunch of strings, or *anding* together a bunch of boolean expressions. Any monoid has a `foldLeft` (or `foldRight`) method, though as previously noted, they may be named slightly differently in different languages.

Our goal is to get to *monads*, see where they come from, and understand how they relate to FP. To define monad, we first need the concept of a natural transformation.

Natural Transformations

To keep things simple, we will not go into all the technical details that make up the definition of natural transformations.[7] My goal here is to give some idea of what a monad is, in the context of category theory, and more importantly, to make clear how they are useful in FP.[8]

We need natural transformations to define monads. Functors, as we know, are functions from one category to another category (for example, from Scal to Scal). But we can change our perspective and build a new category where the objects of the new categories are the functors from the original category.

 Let's say that again. We start with a category *C*. Then we take all functors from *C* to *C*. We make a *new* category whose objects are all those functors from *C* to *C*. Next, we describe what the morphisms are in this new category.

Now we want these functors to be the objects in a new category. To do so, we need morphisms. That is, we need functions between endofunctors that satisfy the rules for

---

7 Natural transformations are complex; you can find more information online (*https://oreil.ly/zTWXb*).

8 If you wish, you can skip what follows, if you are not interested in the theoretical underpinnings of the monad. Later, I will look at monads from a more practical, FP perspective.

morphisms. Natural transformations in the category C correspond to morphisms in this new category of endofunctors. What properties will these morphisms have?

Let us assume we have morphisms from C to C. We call these morphisms natural transformations.

If the following is too abstract for your tastes, feel free to skip to "flatMap and unit" on page 43.

Let us now define an endomorphism. An *endomorphism* is a morphism from a category C to itself. It is just like an ordinary morphism, but the domain category and the codomain category are the same. Let E_1, E_2, and E_3 be three endomorphisms of C. That is, they are three objects of End(C). Let us further suppose we have two morphisms f and g where $E_1 \to E_2$ and g: $E_2 \to E_3$. Then, by the definition of morphism, there exists the composition g o f: $E_1 \to E_3$. This composition is associative. These morphisms, in End(C), are what we call natural transformations in the original category C. In other words, we start with a category C, form the category End(C) and the morphisms of End(C) are natural transformations in C.

To summarize, we have a category we will call End(C), the objects are functors from C to C, and the morphisms are called natural transformations.

Now, how do we get from here to monads?

The trick is to bring in the concept of monoid again. Pick any endomorphism M in End(C). It turns out that M can be given the structure of a monoid. So we have a monoid (M, *, e) in the category End(C). We have a monoid in the category of endofunctors. *This* is a monad. A monoid in the category of endofunctors is how monads appear in category theory.

Remember, every monad is a monoid, but not every monoid is a monad. A monad is a monoid with some extra structure.

The road from a simple category to a monoid in the category of endofunctors is a long one. There are ways of treating monads that are more practical and useful. In fact, there is a way to get from the * operation of the monoid to a function called flatMap and to get from the identity *e* in the monoid to a function called unit. These two functions will provide us with a more practical way of describing monads.

A monad is a monoid and it is also a functor. As a functor, it has a map method (like all functors), and as a monad it also has a flatMap method.

Monads

Now you know where monads come from. What about monads from a practical perspective? Do we need to deal with endofunctors whenever we want to use a monad? And how are monads useful? It turns out that there is a much simpler description of monads in the category Scal (or any other category associated with a programming language). This simpler description has to do with the functions flatMap and unit.

There is a much simpler way of looking at monads. We just need two methods: flatMap and unit.

flatMap and unit

In Scala, flatMap and unit are two functions that can be used to define a monad. They have the following signature:

Scala

```scala
trait Monad[M[_]] {
    def flatMap[A](ma: M[A])(f: A => M[B]): M[B]
    def unit[A](a: A): M[A]
}
```

Here, M[_] is a type constructor. When we put a type A in M[_], we get a new type, M[A] (Think List[A] or Option[A]). So we have ma, an object of type M[A], f, a function from A to M[B] and it returns an object of type M[B]. We will look at some examples, but first, how should you think about monads? The best way to think about monads from an FP perspective is that they provide a context for an object. We can also think of it as adding additional structure to an object. If we have M[A], the M is the context. We can think of it as adding structure to the type A.

If A is any type, M[A] is A with added structure. The added structure is the M.

Let's dive into the practical definition of a monad. We have `flatMap` and `unit`. Let's start with `unit`, since it is simpler. `unit` takes an element of type A and puts it into the context M[A], where M is the monad above. So if M is `Option`, and we start with the string "abc", we get the object `Some("abc")`. This has type `Option[String]`. It's not quite right to say that `Some("abc")` is a string, but we want to say something to this effect. We can say this is a `String` in the context of `Option`. We have *Optionized* the `String`. Or, we can say we have added additional structure.

Now, what about `flatMap`? Let's first consider the function `map` since it's simpler. So we have something like the following.

Let `ma` be of type M[A]. Suppose we have a function f:A → B. Then `ma.map(f)` will give us a value of type M[B]. `map` will basically take the value `ma` out of its context M[A], apply f to it, get a value of type B, and then wrap it in the context to get a value of type M[B].

Suppose now we have `ma` again, a value of type M[A], but we have f: A → M[B]. This happens frequently. M might be `Option` or `List`, for example. If we try `map`, we get: `ma.map(f)`. If you think this through, you will see `map` returns a value of type M[M[B]], and this is probably not what we want. This is where `flatMap` comes into play. `flatMap` maps f over `ma` but then it flattens the result.

Let `ma` be of type M[A]. Let f: A → M[B]. Then `ma.flatMap(f)` will return a value of type M[B], not M[M[B]].

Let's see an example of this.

Scala

```
class User(fname: String {
        def firstName: String  = firstName
}

def getUser(id: Int): Option[User]

val users = List(1,2,3).flatMap(id => getUser(id))
```

If we used `map` here instead of `flatMap`, we would have ended up with a `List` of options of users. `flatMap` maps and then flattens. In general, `flatMap` is useful for chaining together functions that involve monads.

 `flatMap` can be thought of this way: first, apply `map`, then *flatten* the result.

Take the earlier example again.

```
val users = List(1,2,3).flatMap(id => getUser(id))
```

In this example, flatMap first maps a whole number to an option of a user and then flattens the option of the user. Here *flatten* means take the user out of the option.

Incidentally, even though every monad, being a functor, has a map method, you don't have to prove it has a map method. The reason is that if you take flatMap and unit, you can define map. For example, you can get map as follows:

Scala

```
m map g = m flatMap (x => unit(g(x)))
```

If you have a flatMap and a unit, you get map for free.

We can say a monad is a trait (or interface of some kind depending on the programming language) that implements two methods: flatMap and unit. Also, every monad is also a functor, so it must have a map function. The earlier expression shows how to get it from flatMap and unit.

To fully understand monad as it is in category theory would require more work. I hope you have gotten a solid feel for the complexity involved in constructing a monad as well as the more straightforward programming approach in which we model a monad as an interface or trait that implements flatMap and unit.

Also, when somebody asks you what a monad is, you can answer, "It is a monoid in the category of endofunctors," and have some idea what that means.

Conclusion

You have learned what a category is, what the category Scal is, and some examples of how to apply functors, natural transformations, monoids, and monads to your code. I will present more examples in the course of the book. It is important to emphasize here that it is not absolutely necessary to learn category theory before you learn about constructions like functors and monads and how to apply them to your code, but I believe knowing where these constructions come from will give more context and perhaps suggest novel ways of applying them to your code.

CHAPTER 4

Functional Data Structures

Data structures are a foundational concept in computer science. Along with algorithms, they are a staple of what a computer science student or programmer must master. As with the phrase *functional pattern*, *functional data structure* is not an established concept with a consistent definition in the canon of code.

In this book, I will refer to two things as functional data structures.

- Structures used in functional patterns, such as `Option`, `Either`, `Try`, `List`. These are monads.
- Ordinary data structures that are implemented in a functional way so that they don't mutate state, such as a linked list.

In this chapter, we will treat the first kind of functional data structures and then briefly cover some of the ideas surrounding ordinary data structures implemented in a functional way. Before we look at particular data structures, let me mention an idea about functional data structures that has been discussed in the literature. First, there is this quote from Alan Perlis (*https://oreil.ly/5lY7y*):

> It is better to have 100 functions operate on one data structure than to have 10 functions operate on 10 data structures.

Seasoned functional programmers tend to use a small set of data structures: linked lists, arrays, and hash tables, as well as structures such as `Option`, `Either`, and `Try`, to name a few. We will examine these next. I believe the idea behind this quote is that fewer data structures results in more uniformity and simplicity in the codebase. Now, let's look at some data structures that are particularly functional. We will start with `Option`.

The Option Data Structure

I use the word Option as a language neutral term (not as part of any particular programming language). Various programming languages have a version of this data structure and I will give examples of some of them, but first let's flesh out the idea. Our discussion really should start with the null construct. Null is used for a value that might not exist; an optional value or a situation where a value is not known. One problem with null is that if a variable contains an object and the value of that variable is null, and a method is called on that object, the program will throw a null pointer exception. Exceptions break referential transparency and so are frowned upon by functional programmers. Tony Hoare, the inventor of null, said it was his billion-dollar mistake:

> I call it my billion-dollar mistake. It was the invention of the null reference in 1965. At that time, I was designing the first comprehensive type system for references in an object-oriented language (ALGOL W). My goal was to ensure that all use of references should be absolutely safe, with checking performed automatically by the compiler. But I couldn't resist the temptation to put in a null reference, simply because it was so easy to implement. This has led to innumerable errors, vulnerabilities, and system crashes, which have probably caused a billion dollars of pain and damage in the last forty years.[1]

Yet without null, how do we handle a piece of data that is optional or that may not have a value? Well, one of the main problems with null is that it doesn't really have a type. What if we could create a type that represented the case when a value is missing or optional? There is such a thing—it exists in many languages. In those languages in which it doesn't exist, it's not hard to create one. There are a few ways of referring to this type but most of them involve some version of the word Option. We have Optional in Java.[2] Python has something that resembles Option in some ways but does not have the full functionality of Option: the None object. However, it's not hard to construct Option in Python. The idea behind Option is this: suppose we have a method that takes an id and returns a Customer object. What do we do if there is no Customer with the given id?

 We could throw an exception when the Customer is not found, but as I said before, this is not functional, since it breaks referential transparency. If a function throws an exception, it is no longer true that whenever you put in the same input, you get out the same output.

---

1 Hoare, Tony. "Null References: The Billion Dollar Mistake." Historically Bad Ideas. Lecture presented at the QCon, 2009. *https://oreil.ly/sQSnH*.

2 Like many functional constructs, this requires Java 8 or above.

Even if you like exceptions, this example really isn't a suitable case for an exception. An exception refers to something that should not happen, but does. It's arguable that there really isn't any good reason to believe that any old id a system comes up with will correspond to an actual Customer. The situation in which this happens is not uncommon. You might even say it's one of the outcomes that we should expect. So how can we handle this without an exception? Let us consider the Option construct. By Option, I mean a general data structure and not a construct in any particular programming language. An Option usually has two parts: one is a container that holds a value. This is the case where a valid value was computed or obtained somehow. The second part represents the case where no valid value is available. This would be a situation where a language without an Option type might use a null. Let's see an example in Scala. Let's return to the example of retrieving a customer, given an id. In Scala, we can do the following:

Scala

```scala
def getCustomer(id: Int): Option[Customer] = {
    //code which retrieves customer from database.
}
```

This function can return one of two things. In the case where the id corresponds to a customer, the method will return:

```scala
Some(customer)
```

If no customer corresponds to that particular id, the function will return the value:

```scala
None
```

You can then take the necessary action to deal with that situation. If it returns Some(customer), you can then get the customer out of the Some container in a variety of ways. One common way is to use Scala's pattern matching feature. Here is an example of this:

```scala
getCustomer(17) match {
    case Some(customer) => //do something with customer
    case None => //Take action to handle this situation.
}
```

Another, perhaps more common approach is to use one of the higher order functions, such as map, flatMap, or filter. For example:

```scala
val customer = getCustomer(17) map { customer => customer.firstName}
```

The variable customer, in the case where a value was obtained, will contain Some("Peter"). If no customer was found, a None would be returned and the programmer can handle it.

It is important to understand that Some and None are types and therefore the compiler can help to find errors associated with them, unlike null, which occurs at runtime (not compile time).

Suppose now that you had a list of Option objects, each a Some(customer) or a None. And suppose you wanted to change this to a list of customers where you ignore the Nones. Also suppose getCustomers returns a list of options of Customer objects. The Customer object might be a case class that looks like this:

```
case class Customer(id: Int, firstName: String)
```

The list of options of customers looks like this:

```
val customers = List(Some(Customer(1,"Bob")), None, Some(Customer(33, "Lee")),
                                    None, Some(Customer(5, "Rhonda")))
```

Then we could do the following:

```
customers.flatten
```

This would return:

```
List(Customer(1,"Bob"), Customer(33, "Lee"), Customer(5, "Rhonda"))
```

Notice how the Nones were conveniently left out.

Now let's look at some examples in Java.

Java

```
        Optional<User> optUser = findUserById(123);

        optUser.ifPresent(user -> {
                System.out.println("User's name = "
        + user.getName());})
    }
```

In this example, findUserById returns an Optional of a User object if it finds one for the given id. If not, the code in the braces is not executed. The older, pre-Optional way of doing this would have been for findUserById to return a null if a user was not found. The problem with that is that if a method were then called on the User object, which was actually a null, a NullPointerException would be thrown. With the preceding code, which uses Optional, no exception is thrown.

Now, Python does not have an Option class. It does have the None object; this is only half of what makes up an option. It is, however, useful in its own right. You can do things like this:

Python

```
def getUser(id):
    #get user from database

    #if database call fails
    return None
```

Then, you can do this, when calling this function:

```
if getUser(789) is not None:
    #do something
```

You may say that this looks an awful lot like checking for a null, and I would agree with you. If you really want to, you can create an Option class in Python. One way is shown here:

```
class Option:
    def get_or_else(self, default):
        return self.value if isinstance(self, Some) else default

class Some(Option):
    def __init__(self, value):
        self.value = value

class Nothing(Option):
    pass
```

I called this Nothing, because Python already has a None object. This isn't particularly "pythonic," but it's one way to get the job done.

C# also has a version of this idea. It's not exactly an Option, but it is a construct that helps with problems caused by nulls: the Nullable type. With this type, we can represent, in a way that makes it explicit, that a variable may be holding a null value. For a given type, say int, we can form the type:

C#

```
Nullable<int>
```

As you can see, this is a generic type. A shorthand way of writing this is:

```
int?
```

We can also write code like:

```
Nullable<int> n1 = new Nullable<int>(10);
Nullable<int> n2 = null;

if (n1.HasValue) {
    process(n1.Value);
} else {
    //n1 has a null value.
}
```

This is a way of navigating nulls without risking a `NullPointerException`.

The Try Data Structure

While the `Option` construct is useful, and an improvement over nulls, it doesn't give you a clue about why there is no legitimate value. Exceptions do this, but `Option`s do not. `Option`s are a great solution in many situations, but sometimes you need to get some information about what went wrong. The `Try` construct addresses this. Just as `Option` has `Some` and `None`, `Try` has `Success` and `Failure`. `Failure` wraps the exception that was thrown. While we try to avoid exceptions as much as possible in FP, sometimes we cannot avoid it. `Try` is one solution to this problem. Here is some code.

Scala

```
def divide(a: Float, b: Float): Try[Float] = Try(a/b)
```

Then we can do the following:

```
divide(3, 0) match {
  case Success(result) => //do something with result
  case Failure(ex) => println(ex.getMessage)
}
```

Here is an example of `Try` in a for comprehension:

```
def toInt(s: String): Try[Int] = Try(Integer.parseInt(s.trim))

val y = for {
    a <- toInt("9")
    b <- toInt("3.5")
    c <- toInt("6")
} yield a + b + c
```

Notice how well the error case is handled. y will either contain a `Success` wrapping the sum of a, b, and c, or it will contain a `Failure` wrapping an exception.

In this case, the result will be:

```
Failure(java.lang.NumberFormatException: For input string: "3.5")
```

The Either Data Structure

While the `Try` type gives you more information about a failure or exceptional outcome than `Option`, you might wonder if there is a type that gives you more flexibility. The `Either` construct addresses this in the following manner: an `Either` object can be either a `Right` or a `Left`. `Right` is like the `Some` type of `Option`. `Left` is like `None`, except it can wrap any type. Let us consider an example in Scala.

Scala

```scala
def divide(a: Int, b: Int): Either[String, Int] = {
    if (b == 0)
        Left("Can't divide by zero.")
    else
        Right(a/b)
}
```

Then, you can do something like this:

```scala
divide(a, b) match {
    case Left(msg) => //do something with msg
    case Right(res) => //do something with res
}
```

Left and Right can wrap any types. For example, suppose you had two custom types, User and Error:

Scala

```scala
case class User(id: Int, firstName: String)

case class Error(id: Int, text: String)

def getUser(id: Int): Either[Error,User] = {
    //If I retrieve a user from api
    Right(User(id, firstName)

    //else if there is an error
    Left(id, text)
}
```

Then I can do the following:

```scala
getUser(4) match {
    case Right(user) => println(user.firstName)
    case Left(error) => println(error.text)
  }
```

Left can even wrap an exception, if for some reason you find it necessary or prudent to use one and you don't want to use a Try. For example, you might be using a library that throws an exception. It is always possible to catch the exception and return an error type wrapped in Left.

As we get deeper into FP, it will be useful and in some cases necessary to use third-party functional libraries that include many of the structures we have been discussing. You have seen examples in Scala, Java, Python, and C#. These languages vary in how much FP they can do without libraries, but all of them need libraries for some things.[3]

---

3 An exception is the pure FP language, Haskell (*https://oreil.ly/Vh2ej*).

For Java, there are at least two libraries that allow functional constructs. One is called Functional Java (*http://functionaljava.org*) and another is Vavr (*https://www.vavr.io*). I will be giving examples from Vavr. I will always state when some code relies on Vavr. Let us see what Either looks like in Java with Vavr.

Java with Vavr

```
private static Either<String, User> getUser(int id) {
    //code that sucessfully found a user
        return Either.right(user);
    } else {
        return Either.left(String.format("No user found with id  %s", id);
    }
}
```

What about a functional library for Python? One excellent library is OSlash (*https://oreil.ly/6Vd0D*). With OSlash, we can write things in Python like the following:

Python (with OSlash)

```
def get_user(id):
    #successful case yields a user object
    return Right(user)
    #error case returns an error object
    return Left(error)
```

Then we can do this:

```
if isinstance(result,Right):
    #do something with successfull result
else:
    # result is an error
```

Higher Order Functions

Functions that return these functional data structures like Option or Either lend themselves to higher order functions. Let us first see some simple examples of this.

Scala

```
case class User(id, firstName)

val users: List[Option[User]] = List(Some(User(1, "Jack")),
                                    None, Some(User(2, "Andrea")), None, None)
```

The users list could be the result of a function that queries an API and gets options of users back. In those cases in which no User was found for a given id, the function returns a None. To get just the users and not the Nones, we can do this:

```
users.flatten
```

This will return:

```
List(User(1,"Jack"),User(2,"Andrea"))
```

Often, one has a data pipeline of values that they are transforming as they call a bunch of higher order functions. For example, suppose we have a Scala function, getUsers, that returns a list of Either[Error,User], where User has a field called email. Suppose that we want to filter out all users with an *example.com* account. We expect the result to be a List[Either[Error,String]], where the String represents the email address. An imperative approach, which loops through the List, would be a bit messy. Let's see how a functional approach, using higher order functions, greatly simplifies the code. It does this by going directly to the essence of what's going on. Looping is not part of that essence. Let's see some code.

Scala

```
case class User(id: Int, email: String)
case class Error(id: Int, text: String)

def getUsers(): List[Either[Error,User]] =
    List(Right(User(1, "jack@example.com")), Left(Error(4,"user not found")),
        Right(User(2, "andrea@example.com")))
```

Then we can do this:

```
val emails = getUsers().map(either => either.map(u => u.email))
```

Now, emails will contain the following:

```
List(Right(jack@example.com), Left(Error(4,user not found)),
    Right(andrea@example.com))
```

This allows you to drill down into the hierarchy of fields to the one you want.

Monads in for Comprehensions in Scala

As we have seen, things like List, Option, Try, and Either, are monads. One very useful thing you can do with monads in Scala is for comprehensions. Here is an example:

Scala

```
case class Student(id: Int, email: String)
case class FinalGrade(grade: Int)
def getStudent(id: Int): Option[Student] = ???
def getFinalGrade(student: Student): Option[FinalGrade]
```

This function tries to get a User object that corresponds to the given id and if it finds it, it returns Some(User(493, "Alex")), for example. If it does not find it, it returns None. We can now do the following:

```
for {
    student <- getStudent(999) //getStudent returns a monad
```

```
        finalGrade <- getFinalGrade(student) //getFinalGrade returns a monad
    } yield (student,finalGrade)
```

This would return a tuple consisting of an Option of the student and an Option of
the finalGrade. If either of the Options were None, the value of the for comprehension would be None and not the tuple of values. What this does for comprehension,
in effect, is take perfectly functional code and make it look more like traditional
imperative code. In many cases, it results in clearer code. It turns out that a for
comprehension is really just syntactic sugar for a series of flatMap and map calls and
we know that every monad has flatMap and map. Let's start out with a list of Options
of students:

Scala

```
    case class Student(id: Int, email: String)
    val students = List(Some(Student(1,"jack@example.com")), None,
                        Some(Student(2, "andrea@example.com")), None)
```

First, let's assume you just want to get the students out of the options and ignore the
Nones. You can do this with a simple call to flatten:

```
    students.flatten // returns List(Student(1,"jack@example.com"),
        Student(2,"andrea@example.com"))
```

Now, let's say you are just interested in the emails and you want to get a list of them.
You can do the following:

```
    students.flatten.map(student => student.email)

    // This will return List("jack@example.com","andrea@example.com")
```

So we did a flatten and then a map. Sometimes you want to map first, then flatten.
This is precisely what flatMap does. Let's look at an example of this:

```
    students.flatMap(optStudent => opStudent)

    // returns List(Student(1,"jack@example.com"), Student(2,"andrea@example.com"))
```

In this case, for the map, we used the identity function. This made the flatMap call the
same as a call to flatten. We did not use the full power of flatMap. Let's see a more
complicated example. Suppose we have a getStudent function that takes an id and
returns an Option of a Student. This is a good idea since some ids might not refer to
any Student. Here is some code.

```
    def getStudent(id: Int): Option[Student] = {
        id match {
          case 1 => Some(Student(1, "jack@example.com"))
          case 2 => Some(Student(2, "andrea@example.com"))
          case _ => None
        }
    }
```

Let us suppose now that we have a of `ids` and we want to call the previous function on the list somehow, but the function returns an `Option`. We can do the following:

```
List(1,2,3).map(id => getStudent(id))
```

This will return:

```
List(Some(Student(1,jack@example.com)), Some(Student(2,andrea@example.com)), None)
```

This is probably not what we wanted. `flatMap` to the rescue.

```
List(1,2,3).flatMap(id => getStudent(id))
```

Now *this* will return:

```
List(Student(1,jack@example.com), Student(2,andrea@example.com))
```

Perfect! `flatMap` is useful when you have a list (or any monad) and you want to `map` it, but the function that you want to `map` it with returns a monad itself. The `flatten` part of `flatMap` will remove the result from its *container*—that is, its monad.

Traditional Data Structures

Now we will look at traditional data structures, as opposed to functional data structures.

Immutability and History

As with everything functional, immutability is an important piece of the puzzle. What I am calling history here refers to the fact that since we do not change anything, we must copy something that changes (and retain its former state). For example, a stack can be functional if implemented in a certain way. Operations such as `push` would have to make a copy of the stack instead of modifying it in place. This requires, in general, a way of doing quick copies. There are various algorithms for this. There are even databases that follow this paradigm. Datomic, for example, a database created by Rich Hickey, creator of the Clojure language (which has many functional capabilities), is a database that never overwrites data. It keeps a copy of all data and changes made. This is another way that the functional paradigm is becoming more mainstream.

Whether or not a traditional data structure is functional depends on the particular implementation of that data structure.

Laziness

We have mentioned laziness before in connection with what makes a language functional (see "Lazy Evaluation" on page 8). The basic idea is that a function or process is lazy if it is evaluated only when needed. Part of this is the fact that if a function carries out a long computation, the value will be saved or *memoized* and then used the next time it is needed (if possible). This capability is useful in creating efficient functional data structures. Haskell is a lazy language and Scala has a lazy keyword but is not lazy by default. In general, for a language to be partially or fully lazy, it tends to be a language that was explicitly constructed to be, at least in part, functional.

Laziness allows us to wait to evaluate an expression when and only when we need it.

Conclusion

In summary, there are two types of functional data structures. The first is a set of constructs that come from category theory, generally by way of Haskell, and which have a map and flatMap functions, which makes them monads. The second consists of traditional data structures that have been implemented according to the principles mentioned earlier.

CHAPTER 5

More on Immutability

We have seen how important immutability is for FP. This chapter focuses on a number of techniques that help promote immutability. These include recursion, higher order functions, and the combination of monoids with higher order functions. We include in the chapter a new pattern, called *Monoid and Fold*, which represents many seemingly different but actually very similar types of functions. Let us start the chapter with a discussion of mutable and immutable variables.

Immutability is a key property in functional code. The less mutable state a program has, the less the programmer has to keep in mind while writing the program. A large number of programmer errors come from the programmer not being able to keep a mass of changing detail in mind at once. Changing state causes complexity that we must track and manage.

Mutable and Immutable Variables

Almost all programming languages allow you to create a variable, set its value, and then change it at a later time. For an example of one that does not allow this, look at Haskell (*https://oreil.ly/Vh2ej*). A variable that can be modified after it has been set is called a mutable variable.

In imperative and object-oriented programming, mutable variables are ubiquitous. As I have said, in FP, we avoid mutable variables.

Immutability is particularly valuable when dealing with concurrency and parallelism, which we will look at in the next chapter. For now, we will look more closely at the way immutability can be achieved. You have already seen how copying a variable with a new value instead of modifying the variable is useful:

Scala

```scala
case class User(firstName: String, age: Int)
val user = User("Peter", 34)
```

And the next year, we have:

```scala
user.copy("Peter", age = 35)
```

A new instance of User is created instead of just modifying the age variable in the original instance. Copying is part of the way you can implement immutability.

> In functional programs, we prefer to copy an object rather than mutating the variables in the object.

Another way of achieving immutability is with recursion. Let us look at this now.

Recursion

Recursiveness is a property of some functions. Simply put, a function is recursive if somewhere in its body, it calls itself. If you think about it, this seems strange. How can f call f if f hasn't been completely defined yet? You might expect an infinite loop. To be sure, if you define a recursive function badly, you may very well get an infinite loop. I can't resist mentioning this function:

```
def f():
    return f()
```

This is the simplest recursive function. What happens when we call this function? If you are not sure, try it. In Chapter 1, we saw the following example of recursion.

Java

```java
void f(int i) {
if (i > 99) {
return;
}
else {
System.out.println( i)
return f(i+1)
}
}
```

In this example, no state is mutated.

Let us now consider something more substantial.

A Linked List Example

We will look at some code written in a common, mutable way and see how we can use a functional approach to make it all immutable. The following code defines a linked list and then adds a node to it. First, the imperative approach. Notice how it uses the var keyword, which denotes a mutable variable in Scala.

Scala

```scala
case class Node[A](data: A, var next: Option[Node[A]])

def nodeAppend[A](node: Node[A], toAppend: Node[A]): Node[A] = {
    if (node.next == None) {
        node.next = Some(toAppend)
    } else {
        var current = node
        while (current.next != None) {
            current = current.next.getOrElse(current)
        }
        current.next = Some(toAppend)
    }
    node
}
```

Notice how the variable next is a var, which makes it a mutable variable, and the nodeAppend method continually updates the current variable, which is also a var. We would like to replace this code with vals, instead of vars. This will ensure we cannot mutate any variables. To accomplish this, we will bring in a new, higher order function called fold. fold takes an initial value, and then a function that tells you how to combine two of the values. Here is a simple example that lets you add up the numbers in a list:

Scala

```scala
val lst = List(1,2,3,4,5)

lst.fold(0)((m,n) => m + n) //This evaluates to 15
```

fold uses currying.[1] fold is used when you know how to combine two things and you want to combine a bunch of those things. Let's see how we can use fold, along with copy and recursion to make the earlier linked list example immutable.

---

1 See "Currying" on page 106 for a definition of currying.

```
case class Node[A](data: A, next: Option[Node[A]])

def nodeAppend[A](node: Node[A], toAppend: Node[A]): Node[A] =
  node.next.fold(node.copy(next = Some(toAppend)))(
      nxt => node.copy(next = Some(nodeAppend(nxt, toAppend))))
```

This might appear confusing at first sight. Once you get used to it, you can appreciate that it is shorter, more concise, and does not mutate any state! This is a common use of fold and recursion. Let's look at some more examples. In Java 8, the stream construct has a function called reduce. This is similar to reduce in other languages and is basically like fold. Here is a simple example of adding up numbers using reduce.

Java

```
List<Integer> integers = Arrays.asList(1, 2, 3, 4, 5);
Integer sum = integers.stream()
  .reduce(0, (a, b) -> a + b);
```

The sum variable will be equal to the sum of the numbers, 15. As we begin to think in terms of reducing and folding instead of looping through collections and mutating state, we will notice that the level of abstraction of our code has increased. Our code is less like the language of the machine and more like that of a person. Let's look at some more examples. If we have a function called add, as in the following example:

Java

```
public static int add(int a, int b) {
      return a + b;
}
```

in a class called Utils, then we can do this:

```
List<Integer> integers = Arrays.asList(1, 2, 3, 4, 5);
Integer sum = integers.stream()
  .reduce(0, Utils::add);
```

In the java.util.stream package is a class called Collectors. It has a method called summingInt. With this we can do the following:

Java

```
List<Integer> integers = Arrays.asList(1, 2, 3, 4, 5);
Integer sum = integers.stream()
  .collect(Collectors.summingInt(Integer::intValue));
```

Java 8 has a variety of expressive constructs for raising the level of abstraction in your code. These work well for numbers. There is also a function called summingLong, which does the same thing for Longs. What about for objects? Consider the following code:

Java

```
public class Item {

    private int id;
    private Integer price;

    public Item(int id, Integer price) {
        this.id = id;
        this.price = price;
    }

    // Standard getters and setters
}
```

Let's create some Item objects:

```
List<Integer> integers = Arrays.asList(1, 2, 3, 4, 5);
Integer sum = integers.stream()
  .collect(Collectors.summingInt(Integer::intValue));

public class Item {

    private int id;
    private Integer price;

    public Item(int id, Integer price) {
        this.id = id;
        this.price = price;
    }

    // Standard getters and setters
}

Item item1 = new Item(1, 10);
Item item2 = new Item(2, 15);
Item item3 = new Item(3, 25);
Item item4 = new Item(4, 40);
```

Then we can do the following, using our add function from earlier:

```
Integer sum = items.stream()
  .map(x -> x.getPrice())
  .reduce(0, Utils::add);
```

Perhaps a better approach—and one that doesn't depend on the Utils::add function—is using a lambda expression, (a, b) -> a + b:

```
Integer sum = items.stream()
  .map(item -> item.getPrice())
  .reduce(0, (a, b) -> a + b);
```

This is elegant, compact, easy to read, and does not mutate any state.

Combined with a simple regular expression, there is no end to expressiveness we can achieve. Consider the following `string` examples. Say you have a space-delimited string of words, each of which contains a number within it. We want to add those numbers together. The `filter` function filters out those strings that satisfy a certain predicate, here specified by a regular expression. This allows us to do the following:

```
String string = "Item1 10 Item2 25 Item3 30 Item4 45";

Integer sum = Arrays.stream(string.split(" "))
    .filter((s) -> s.matches("\\d+"))
    .mapToInt(Integer::valueOf)
    .sum();
```

Notice how much this is doing in so few lines of code. Also, through these examples, we can begin to see the role of streams in FP.

One way of characterizing FP is as the transforming of immutable data, as it moves through streams.

Whether those streams are explicitly streams, of the sort we find in Java 8 or Scala, or are simply collections of data, like linked lists or arrays, the idea is the same; we are creating pipelines of immutable data and at each stage we are transforming that data. After a while, you may find that looking at data processing this way is easy and fun, and possibly even less error prone than approaches that loop through data and mutate variables.

Using higher order functions is often a more concise and compact way of treating a collection of values than looping through the collection and mutating state.

Let us look at some more examples of how recursion and higher order functions come together to create pipelines of data. Let's say we want a function that takes a list of positive integers, and for each integer n, prints a row of the character a, n-squared times. Seems a bit artificial, but perhaps it's a subroutine in a graphics program. In Python, we could do the following:

Python

```
def print_row_of_as(ints):
        for k in map(lambda n: n*n, ints):
            print('a' * k)
```

In Java or Scala, for example, map would be a higher order function. In Python, it's actually a class, but it still works like a higher order function. In fact, a principle in FP is that in the functional world, the distinction between object and function starts to break down. In Python, we can think of map or filter as functions or objects. I tend to think of things as functions, whenever possible.

In many modern languages, functions *are* objects. The other way around, seeing objects as functions, takes a bit more work.

Here is one way we might achieve this in Python. Suppose we want to create a Square class (think *x*-squared, not the shape). We can use the built-in function __call__, to do the following (we will omit all but what we need to make the point):

```
class Square:
    def __call__(self,n):
        return n * n
```

Then we could do this:

```
f = Square()
print(f(3))
```

This will print out 9. Now, what is Square? Is it a class or a function? Technically, at the level of syntax, it's a class. More generally speaking, it is a function, and it was very easy to turn the class into a function.

In Scala, we have the apply function. From a higher-level perspective, we can conceive of functions as objects and objects as functions.

Now let us return to examples of how recursion and higher order functions work together. Let's focus on more Python examples. Python does not have a fold function, but it does have a reduce function. This comes from the functools package. A simple example that adds a bunch of numbers could be written as follows:

```
from functools import reduce
reduce(lambda m,n: m+n, [1,2,3,4,5])
```

This will return 15. Interestingly, we can do the same thing with strings. In the case of strings, adding is concatenation. We have:

```
from functools import reduce
reduce(Lambda s,t: s+t, ["a","b","c","d"])
```

Let's look at some other basic uses of recursion with some more Python examples. First, let's compute the length of a list recursively. To do this, I would like to use the list's `tail` function, which returns all but the first element in a new list. Sadly, Python has no such function. No worries—in Python 3, we can do the following (very elegant) thing:

```
def tail(lst):
    _, *tail = lst
    return tail
```

The _ could have been named `head`, but we don't need it in the function. So _ anonymously holds the first element of `lst`. The * causes `tail` to contain the rest of what's in `lst`. Now, we can write our `length` function:

```
def length(lst):
    if lst == []:
        return 0
    else:
        return 1 + length(tail(lst))
```

Let's use the same idea to `sum` a list of integers:

```
def sum(lst):
    if lst == []:
        return 0
    else:
        return lst[0] + sum(tail(lst))
```

A more "pythonic" definition of `tail` would be:

```
def tail(lst):
    return [1:len(lst)]
```

As we have seen, recursion is a useful way of avoiding the mutation of state. You may know that recursion relies on continually pushing values on the stack and then popping them when necessary. If you put too many values on the stack, you may get a stack overflow error. Even though recursion depends on the stack, the definition of recursion doesn't mention the stack explicitly. In fact, it is possible in many instances to have a recursive function that doesn't rely on pushing values onto the stack. What happens is that in these instances, the compiler is able to rewrite the recursive function as a loop. When this happens, this is called a tail recursive function.

Tail Recursion

A tail recursive function is a recursive function in which the last line of the body of the function is the calling of the function itself.

Let's look at a simple example.

Scala

```scala
def printToZero(n: Int): Int = {
        if (n < 0)
            return 0
        println(n)
        printToZero((n-1))
    }
```

This function starts at n and prints every number less than n up to and including 0. In the body of the function, the last thing to be called is the function itself. *That* is a tail recursive function. Here is another example. It computes the greatest, common divisor of two positive integers.

Scala

```scala
def gcd(a: Int, b: Int): Int =
    if (b == 0) a else gcd(b, a % b)
```

How does a tail recursive function differ from an ordinary recursive function as far as performance is concerned? Since the tail recursive function calls itself, you might think it necessarily requires a stack to implement it. It turns out that ordinary recursive functions do require putting the argument on the stack but tail recursive functions can be rewritten, by the compiler or preprocessor, in a way that uses a simple for loop. There is thus no possibility of a stack overflow exception.

Let's look at some more examples. What would a tail recursive version of factorial look like? Let's first look at the straightforward version of a recursive factorial.

Scala

```scala
def factorial(n: Int): Int = {
    if (n == 0)
        1
    else
        n * factorial(n-1)
}
```

How can we make this tail recursive? Here is one way:

```scala
def factorial(n: Int): Int = {
        def fact(k: Int, result: Int): Int = {
            if (k == 0)
                return result
            else
                return fact(k-1, k * result)
        }
        fact(n, 1)
    }
```

In this case, `factorial` defines a function within its body and this inner function is tail recursive. The `factorial` function is not technically tail recursive, since it doesn't call itself at all, but it's just as good since the stack implementation is replaced with a `for` loop in the body of the function.

Let's look at some more examples. Here is a tail recursive version of `fibonacci`. First, let's see the usual, non–tail recursive version.

Java

```
int fibonacci(int n) {
    if (n == 0) {
        return 0
    } else if (n == 1) {
        return 1
    }
    return fibonacci(n-2) + fibonacci(n-1)
}
```

This sort of recursion is called tree-recursion because the *shape* of this computation is a binary tree. As is well known, the performance is terrible. It is not hard to see why this is. The same computations are repeated over and over. One solution is to write a tail recursive version of this function. Here it is in Java:

Java

```
int fib(int n, int a, int b )
    {
        if (n == 0)
            return a;
        if (n == 1)
            return b;
        return fib(n - 1, b, a + b);
    }

int fibonacci(int n) {
    return fib(n, 0, 1)
}
```

This is particularly elegant in Python, due to the default values a and b.

Python

```
def fib(n, a = 0, b = 1):
    if n == 0:
        return a
    if n == 1:
        return b
    return fib(n - 1, b, a + b)
```

One can achieve this elegance in JavaScript as well:

JavaScript

```javascript
function fib(n, a = 0, b = 1)
{
    if (n == 0){
        return a;
    }
    if (n == 1){
        return b;
    }
    return fib(n - 1, b, a + b);
}
```

Let us now try to add up the elements in the `array` in a tail recursive way.

Python

```python
def arrSum(array, size, sum = 0):
        if size == 0:
                return sum

        return arrSum(array, size - 1,
                        sum + array[size - 1])
```

Java

```java
int arraySumHelper(int []array, int size, int sum)
{
    if (size == 0)
        return sum;

    return arraySumHelper(array, size - 1, sum + array[size - 1]);
}

int arraySum(int[] array) {
    return arraySumHelper(array, array.length, 0);
}
```

JavaScript

```javascript
function arrSum(array, size, sum = 0)
{
    if (size == 0)
        return sum;

    return arrSum(array, size - 1, sum + array[size - 1]);
}
```

In Scala, if you place the annotation @tailrec above a function, it ensures the implementation is tail recursive. If it is not, the compiler throws an error.

The process of rewriting a function to take advantage of tail recursion is called *tail call optimization* (TCO).

Java does not directly support TCO at the compiler level.

More Examples of the Power of fold in Scala

We will start with some simple examples. Suppose we have a max function that takes two numbers and returns the larger one. We want to apply it to a list of numbers. Let's see how we can do this using max and the fold function.

Scala

```scala
val lst = List(1,2,3,4,5)
val m = lst.fold(1)(_ max _)
```

In one line of code, we can sum up a list of numbers without a for loop. Concise, yet easy to read.

Let's say we have a list of words and want the longest word:

```scala
def getLongestWord(words: List[String]): String =
    words.reduce((a,b) => if (a.length > b.length) a else b)
```

How about a simple product function that takes a list of integers?

```scala
def product(lst: List[Int]): Int = lst.fold(1)(_ * _)
```

Let's implement the length of a List, using fold. I will call it count and it will take a List[Any].

Scala

```scala
def count(list: List[Any]): Int =
    list.foldLeft(0)((sum,_) => sum + 1)
```

Let's look at some more complex examples. Try to figure out what each one does. I will name the functions f1, f2, etc., so as not to give away what they do:

```
def f1(list: List[Double]): Double =
  list.foldLeft(0.0)(_+_) / list.foldLeft(0.0)((r,c) => r+1)

def f2[A](list: List[A]): A =
  list.foldLeft[A](list.head)((_, c) => c)

def f3[A](list: List[A]): A =
  list.foldLeft( (list.head, list.tail.head) )((r, c) => (r._2, c) )._1

def f4[A](list: List[A]): List[A] =
  list.foldLeft(List[A]())((r,c) => c :: r)

def f5[A](list: List[A]): List[A] =
  list.foldLeft(List[A]()) { (r,c) =>
    if (r.contains(c)) r else c :: r
  }
```

A Connection Between fold and Monoids

We learned about monoids in Chapter 3 and it turns out that there is a close connection between monoids and the fold function. This is an area where higher order functions and data structures come together to produce a means of raising abstraction in your code that has the ultimate result of simplification.

Higher order functions and functional data structures can often come together to create abstractions that can simplify your code.

Let us start by recalling the definition of a monoid.

As mentioned in Chapter 3, a semigroup is a set with an associative operation on it. If a semigroup has an identity element, which means an element *e*, in the semigroup, with the property that:

$$e * x = x * e = x$$

For all elements *x* in the semigroup, the semigroup is called a monoid.

Let us start by implementing a Monoid trait in Scala. This will be a barebones implementation for learning purposes. Then we will examine its connection to the fold function:

```
trait Monoid[A] {
    def combine(x: A, y: A): A
```

```
        def empty: A
    }
```

`combine` is a binary operation and `empty` represents things like 0, the empty string, `false` or `true` (depending on what combine does), and generally, that object that when combined with any other object gives the same object back. Let us look at some instances.

```
    class IntMonoid extends Monoid[Int] {
        def combine(m: Int, n: Int): Int = m + n
        def empty: Int = 0
    }
```

Now, what does this have to do with `fold`? You may observe that this trait offers *exactly* what we need for `fold`. We need a way to combine two objects to get a third one and a starting object, which essentially has no effect when combined with other objects. If we had wanted to, we could have called `Monoid Foldable`. Let us apply fold to a list of integers using the `IntMonoid` class:

```
    val monoid = new IntMonoid
    val lst = (1 to 1000).toList
    lst.fold(monoid.empty)(combine)
```

We see here that monoids go right to the heart of the matter of folding. Notice, also, how little we have to change if we want to concatenate strings instead of adding integers. We can do the following:

```
    class StringMonoid extends Monoid[String] {
        def combine(s: String, t: String): String =  s + t
        def empty: String = ""
    }

    val lst = List("a","b","c","d")
    val monoid = new StringMonoid
    lst.fold(monoid.empty)(monoid.combine)
```

And now let's and together a bunch of booleans.

```
    class AndMonoid extends Monoid[Boolean] {
        def combine(x: Boolean, y: Boolean): Boolean = x && y
        def empty: Boolean = true
    }

    val lst = List(false, true, true, true)
    val monoid = new AndMonoid
    lst.fold(monoid.empty)(monoid.combine) // returns false
```

Similarly, with or:

```
    class OrMonoid extends Monoid[Boolean] {
        def combine(x: Boolean, y: Boolean): Boolean = x || y
        def empty: Boolean = false
    }
```

```
val lst = List(false, true, true, true)
val monoid = new AndMonoid
lst.fold(monoid.empty)(monoid.combine) // returns true
```

Some more examples follow. It is noteworthy how many different patterns of computation are instances of the Monoid concept.

```
class ProductMonoid extends Monoid[Double]{
    def combine(x: Double, y: Double): Double = x * y
    def empty: Double = 1.0
}

val lst = List(1.0, 2.0, 3.0, 4.0)
monoid = new ProductMonoid[Double]
lst.fold(monoid.empty)(monoid.combine) //returns 24.0
```

You may notice we can compute factorial this way:

```
class IntProductMonoid extends Monoid[Int] {
    def combine(x: Int, y: Int): Int = x * y
    def empty: Int = 1
}

monoid = new ProductMonoid

def factorial(n: Int): Int =
    (1 to n).toList.fold(monoid.empty)(monoid.combine)
```

Or the *sum version* of factorial—adding up the numbers from 1 to *n*. Such a number is called the _n_th triangular number. The triangular numbers start off: 1, 3, 6, 10, 15, and so forth.

```
class IntTriangularMonoid extends Monoid[Int] {
    def combine(x: Int, y: Int): Int = x + y
    def empty: Int = 0
}

monoid = new IntTriangularMonoid

def nthTriangularNumber(n: Int) =
    (1 to n).toList.fold(monoid.empty)(monoid.combine)
```

Remember that combine has to be associative. That is, for all x, y, and z, we have to have:

```
combine(combine(x,y), z) == combine(x, combine(y,z))
```

Also notice that all of these examples involve monoid.empty and monoid.combine. We could define the following general function for a given monoid m:

```
def f[A](lst: List[A]): A = lst.fold(m.empty)(m.combine)
```

This one, general function is general enough to express all the previous examples! We might even say that all of these examples are the same function, parameterized by various monoids.

More with Higher Order Functions

fold is a higher order function. It takes a function as one of its parameters. The general pattern is that we have a List or some other collection object. We call a higher order function f on the collection and pass in a function that does something to the elements of the collection. Let's look at a few examples of the simplest of all higher order functions, map. map is usually called on a container like a List or even an Option. In fact, it can be called on any monad. As I explained in Chapter 3, every monad is a functor and a functor always has a map function.

Without map, anytime you want to modify the elements of a collection, you would have to iterate through the collection and mutate state while doing so. Let's look at some examples.

Let's say we want to take the first n positive integers, square each one, and add them all together. Here is a Scala function that does this:

Scala

```
def sumOfSquares(n: Int) = (1 to n).toList.map(m => m*m).sum
```

The level of abstraction is higher than an imperative version of this and it is easier to read once you get used to the idea. We could have used fold instead of sum if we wanted to emphasize common patterns through the program. That would look like this:

```
def sumOfSquares(n: Int) = (1 to n).toList.map(m => m*m).fold(0)(_ + _)
```

The goal is to maximize both legibility and concision. I mentioned that we could use the fold function to emphasize common structure in the program. The idea here is that all the instances of, say, fold in a program are instances of a common structure. The earlier map examples also have another common structure. Because they are map examples, there is a functor lurking in the room. If you do this thing often enough, you will look at a function like sumOfSquares and immediately think *Functor* and *Monoid*. First, let's write a trait for Functor and then express sumOfSquares with it.

```
trait Functor[F[_]] {
  def map[A, B](fa: F[A])(f: A => B): F[B]
}
```

Here F is the functor. The map function takes an element of F[A], a function f: A => B, and returns an element of F[B]. Think of F as a List, an Option, or another Functor (monads will do since they are also functors).

Now let's create a listFunctor:

```scala
val listFunctor: Functor[List] = new Functor[List] {
    def map[A, B](ls: List[A])(f: A => B) = ls.map(x => f(x))
}

def sumOfSquares(n: Int): Int =
    listFunctor.map((1 to n).toList)(m => m*m).fold(0)(_ + _)
```

So sumOfSquares turns out to be a combination of a Functor and a use of fold. I might not want to sum squares, outside of an instructional context, so let's think of something I might want to do. How about identifying whether a positive integer is a prime? Recall that a prime is a positive integer that has exactly two factors.[2] How can we express this functionally?

```scala
private def isPrime(n: Int): Boolean =
    (2 to (n - 1)).forall(n % _ != 0)
```

forall here is a higher order function that ensures the predicate it takes as an argument is true for every number in (2 to (n - 1)). This effectively says that every number between 2 and n - 1 inclusive is not 0 mod n. In other words, every number fails to divide n. This function works but there is a mathematical undesirability about it. Can you spot it? Hint: It's something about the (2 to (n - 1)). The following better version makes the problem more explicit:

```scala
def isPrime(n: Int): Boolean =
    (2 to math.sqrt(n).toInt).forall(n % _ != 0)
```

The reason this is better and the reason that, as an algorithm, the first version is not so great is that it checks all the integers up to one less than the number. But consider this: if k divides n, then either k or n/k is less than or equal to sqrt(n). If both were greater than sqrt(n), then their product would be greater than n. But their product *is* n. So either k or n/k is less than or equal to sqrt(n). Therefore, when we are checking if an integer is prime, we just have to check up to the square root of the number.

 Here is a mathematical observation. When checking if a number is prime, you only have to check divisors up to (and including) the square root of that number.

---

2 The usual definition says that a prime is a positive integer with at most two factors and then says 1 is an exception. But 1 *really* is not a prime. Every positive integer can be written as a product of prime powers in a way that is unique, up to ordering of the factors. If 1 were a prime, we would have 1 = 1 × 1 and also 1 = 1 × 1 × 1, etc. So 1 behaves differently from the primes.

As an example of a function that tells us if an integer is prime, and does so in a functional style, the isPrime function is a beautiful example. No mutation and its use of the higher order function forall makes it concise.

From map to flatMap

We saw in Chapter 3 that while a functor always has a map function, a monad always has both a map *and* a flatMap function. Let's look at some more flatMap examples. First, suppose we have a User class and a getUser function that returns a User, given an id.

```
case class User(id: Int, firstName: String)

def getUser(Id: Int): User = ???
```

Using ??? in Scala is a way of telling the compiler, *I am not finished yet, but still compile.* It's useful while writing code. Suppose getUser returns a null, if the id doesn't correspond to a User.

And let's say we want to get the users that correspond to the ids 1 to 10 and from them we want to get their first names. We can do the following:

Scala

```
(1 to 10).toList.map(id => getUser(id))
```

This will produce a List of elements, each of which is either a User or a null. So first, let's improve on the null. Of course, we can and should use an Option here. Then there will be no chance of a NullPointerException and the compiler will check that everything is alright. Now we have:

```
case class User(id: Int, firstName: String)

def getUser(id: Int): Option[User]
```

When we evaluate this:

```
(1 to 3).map(id => getUser(id))
```

we will get something like this:

```
List(Some(User(1, "Carl")), None, Some(User(3,"Mary")))
```

However, we don't want the Somes and we don't want the Nones. We just want the first names of those users that correspond to the ids. There is a function that will give us just that:

```
(1 to 3).flatMap(id => getUser(id))
```

This will return the following:

```
List(User(1,"Carl"), User(3, "Mary"))
```

Perfect! What `flatMap` is doing is first mapping and then flattening. Flattening means removing an object from the functor containing it and discarding the failure case. In the case of `Options`, the failure case is `None`. To get the bigger picture of `flatMap`, let us look at its signature. It generally is defined within a monad. Remember, we can define a monad, loosely speaking, as a trait or interface that implements `map` and `flatMap`:

```
trait Monad[M[_]] {
    def flatMap[A,B](ma: M[A])(f: A => M[B]): M[B]
}
```

Recall that a monad provides *context* to an object. You can think of it as a container around an object that has a `map` and `flatMap` function. The function `f` in the preceding `flatMap` signature returns a `B` object inside of the context `M`. If you `map` over it, you will end up with, say, a list of `M[B]`s. You may want to access the `B`s directly; this is where `flatMap` is useful. We'll look at a few more `flatMap` examples. Since `flatMap` maps and flattens, and a string is a list of characters, what do you think the following does?

```
val ls = List("Hello", "World")
ls.flatMap(s => s.toUpperCase)
```

It evaluates to `List(H, E, L, L, O, W, O, R, L, D)`. It maps each word to uppercase and then flattens them.

Let us look at some more examples. Suppose you have a list of integers and you want to replace the list with a list that contains each integer appearing twice. So `List(1,2,3)` would `map` to `List(1,1,2,2,3,3)`. Here is some code for this:

```
def doubleUpInts(ls: List[Int]): List[Int] =
    ls.flatMap(i => List(i, i))
```

To see why `flatMap` is necessary, let's see what would happen if we replaced `flatMap` in the last example with `map`. We would have:

```
def doubleUpInts(ls: List[Int]) = ls.map(i => List(i, i))
```

Notice I didn't include the return type. That is because if I put `List[Int]` as the return type, the program would fail to compile. The true return type of this function is `List[List[Int]]`. `flatMap` *flattens* this down to `List[Int]`.

Conclusion

We know that immutability is one of the most important features in FP. In this chapter, we saw a number of techniques for keeping the state in our programs immutable. Recursion allows us to not loop through variables and mutate state. Instead, for functions in which we would have previously mutated state, we can now call the same function we are in with different arguments. We also have to continually check some condition that the arguments satisfy and return at the right moment. If we don't do this, we could have an infinite loop on our hands.

We do have to be careful of stack overflows, even with the large amounts of ram our machines have. When dealing with huge amounts of data, this is always a possibility. When possible, we can make our recursive functions *tail recursive*, which means the last thing the function does in its body is call itself. These functions can be optimized and reimplemented with a for loop instead of using the stack.

 Beware of stack overflow when using a recursive function on a large dataset. Use tail recursive functions when possible.

We have also seen how higher order functions can help us avoid state mutating in for and while loops. In the process of going through examples, we saw how from one pattern, in this case using a Functor and the fold function, we could produce many seemingly different functions. We wrote down one function, which for any given monoid m, produced a new function. Here is that function:

Scala

```scala
def f[A](lst: List[A]): A = lst.fold(m.empty)(m.combine)
```

This is in fact a pattern, which I would like to call the Monoid and Fold pattern.

Finally, we looked at the higher order function flatMap in more detail. This is a critical function because along with map, it comprises the monad.

I encourage the reader to try to come up with more patterns like Monoid and Fold. Perhaps start with a monad instead of a monoid, and try various higher order functions in addition to fold. New patterns can be discovered.

CHAPTER 6

Questions of Concurrency

I am going to start this chapter with a sentence that sounds a bit mystical: with no mutation of state, we can ignore time.

Let us unpack this. First of all, what does time have to do with mutation of state, or with programming for that matter? Time enters programming when we have a set of processes that need to be executed in a particular order.

Let's consider the following example.[1] Consider two functions. The first takes x to $x + 1$. The second takes x to $x \times x$. Let's set x to 10. Now let's imagine running these two functions in parallel. What would the answer be? Would you be surprised that there are five possible correct answers? Let's break this down. Let $P1 = x \rightarrow x \times x$ and $P2 = x \rightarrow x + 1$:

- If $P1$ sets x to 100 and then $P2$ sets 100 to 101, we get 101.

- If $P2$ sets x to 11 and then $P1$ sets 11 to 121, we get 121.

- $P2$ changes 10 to 11 between the two times that P1 accesses the value of x during the evaluation of $x \times x$. In this case, we get 110.

- $P2$ accesses x. Then $P1$ sets x to 100. Then $P2$ sets x. This gives 10.

- $P1$ accesses x twice. Then $P2$ sets x to 11. Then $P1$ sets x. This gives 100.

Which is the correct answer? 101, 121, 110, 10, or 100? Well, that depends on what the programmer intended. The point is that if we just let $P1$ and $P2$ run in parallel, we can't be sure which answer will be returned. The reason is that the computer can decide to evaluate these two functions in any of the earlier orders.

---

1 This example was taken from *Structure and Interpretation of Computer Programs* (*https://oreil.ly/WoaYy*) by Harold Abelson, Jerry Sussman, and Julie Sussman (MIT Press).

When state is mutated, the order in which processes are run matters.

What can be done about this? The ideal is to have no shared, mutable state. What is shared, mutable state? *Shared* means at least two different threads are accessing it and *mutable* means it changes. This is where problems can occur. Without shared, mutable state, the order in which functions are called does not matter. If it is not possible to avoid shared, mutable state, having it encapsulated is the next best thing. This idea here is to keep the shared, mutable state in as small a region as possible.

One programming model that is particularly well suited to encapsulated, mutable, shared state is the actor model. We will examine that next.

From the Wikipedia page for the actor model (*https://oreil.ly/rYgis*):

> The actor model in computer science is a mathematical model of concurrent computation that treats actor as the universal primitive of concurrent computation. In response to a message it receives, an actor can: make local decisions, create more actors, send more messages, and determine how to respond to the next message received. Actors may modify their own private state, but can only affect each other indirectly through messaging (removing the need for lock-based synchronization).

Lock-based synchronization is when you allow only one thread at a time to access a piece of code. That is one of the main traditional approaches to the problem of shared, mutable state.

The actor model provides a high level abstraction for writing concurrent and distributed systems. It alleviates the developer from having to deal with explicit locking and thread management, making it easier to write correct concurrent and parallel systems.

Actors were defined in a 1973 paper by Carl Hewitt but have been popularized by the Erlang language and used with great success to build highly concurrent and reliable telecom systems at Ericsson. The Akka actor library is a Scala/Java library that has borrowed some of its syntax from Erlang. Actors are in some way like objects but they tend to be at a higher level of abstraction. What this means is that actors tend to represent cross-cutting concerns like Logging and Security rather than OOP objects like User and Message, though they can represent the latter as well. The main thing to remember about actors is that they make concurrency much easier, in many cases.

So how do actors work? The fundamental idea is that each actor has its own *mailbox*, which is a container that holds a linear collection of messages. Other actors send these messages to the actor and the messages are deposited in the actor's mailbox.

Then the actor processes the messages one at a time. The actor also receives a pointer to the sender in case it wants to return a message. The messages are immutable. Sending around mutable messages would open up the model to the difficult task of managing changing state, especially when various threads are touching that state.

Since the messages are immutable and the messages are processed one at a time, there is no possibility of corrupted, mutable, shared state.

The Akka library, a library closely integrated with Scala, provides actors and their infrastructure. With regard to performance, Akka actors can handle 50 million messages per second on a single machine! Part of what makes this possible is the immutability of the messages. In Scala, we use case objects to represent the messages.[2]

The basic idea is that we create actors and then send messages to them, telling them to take some action. Sending a message is a little bit like calling a method on an object. In fact, some early OOP languages, notably Smalltalk, passed messages instead of calling methods. It is a viable alternative to methods when creating an object-oriented language, though methods are far more popular.

The general approach to using actors is to consider what you are modeling from the perspective of communication, decide what the main players are and how they communicate with each other, and create actors to represent these players.

Let's look at some code that implements a miniature version of the game Pong. There are two kinds of actors: typed and untyped. Typed actors are a more recent standard. We will use the untyped actors for our examples because it is simpler and we can focus more on the fundamental ideas. You will see classes such as Actor, ActorRef, and ActorSystem in the following code. We will explain these afterward.

Scala

```
case object PingMessage
case object PongMessage
case object StartMessage
case object StopMessage

class Ping(pong: ActorRef) extends Actor {
  var count = 0
  def incrementAndPrint { count += 1; println("ping") }
```

---

2 See the Appendix for more on case objects.

```
    def receive = {
      case StartMessage =>
          incrementAndPrint
          pong ! PingMessage
      case PongMessage =>
          incrementAndPrint
          if (count > 99) {
            sender ! StopMessage
            context.stop(self)
          } else {
            sender ! PingMessage
          }
    }
  }


  class Pong extends Actor {
    def receive = {
      case PingMessage =>
          println("  pong")
          sender ! PongMessage
      case StopMessage =>
          context.stop(self)
    }
  }


  object PingPongTest extends App {
    val system = ActorSystem("PingPongSystem")
    val pong = system.actorOf(Props[Pong], name = "pong")
    val ping = system.actorOf(Props(new Ping(pong)), name = "ping")
    // start them going
    ping ! StartMessage
  }
  ping ! PongMessage
```

That last line, `ping ! PongMessage`, means we are sending the message `PongMessage` to the `ping` actor. This gets the ball rolling, as it were.

We see in the preceding definition of the `Ping` class that there is a parameter called `pong` that has type `ActorRef` (and not `Actor`). This is an immutable handle to an actor that may or may not reside on the same host.

We also see the class `ActorSystem`. This is the context of the `Actor` and it is the `ActorSystem` that creates new actors.

The Akka library provides for two fundamental concepts: actors and streams. We have looked briefly at actors and now we will look at streams. Incidentally, streams are implemented by way of actors.

Streams

Let us consider streams now. A stream, generally, is a potentially infinite, sequential container for data. It allows us to modify and process chunks of data as those chunks "move" through the stream. A stream is, in a way, a generalization of an ordinary collection. From a functional perspective, the idea is this: on the one hand, we could have an object in memory, and that object's fields are mutated in time. This is the standard imperative or object-oriented paradigm of mutating state. With a stream, in a functional program, we have a memory area, objects coming into the stream, and objects leaving the stream.

 Instead of mutating state, we can think of later objects as being a later evolutional stage of a previous object without any notion of time.

Think of it as similar to the example of a variable x that ranges over the positive integers. We could think of x as changing as time flows from $t = 1$, $t = 2$, $t = 3$, etc. Or we could think of x as a function that exists all at one time. In this case, nothing has changed. A stream can be thought of in the same way. It is a matter of perspective. There are many streaming libraries and they vary in design and purpose. We will look at a few across a few different programming languages.

Akka Streams

So how do Akka streams work? Akka streams are actually implemented with Akka actors under the covers. To start with, since Akka streams are built on actors, we need an ActorSystem just as we have in the case of actors.

Scala

```
implicit val system: ActorSystem = ActorSystem("StreamExample")
```

Let us also import the necessary stream-related classes:

```
import akka.stream._
import akka.stream.scaladsl._
```

A stream, in Akka, is made of three fundamental parts: the Source, the Flow, and the Sink.

Source

The source of a stream is what it sounds like. This is where the data enters the stream. Akka provides many prebuilt sources. Here is a simple one:

Scala

```scala
val source = Source(1 to 1000)
```

It is important to point out that the variable `source` here does not actually contain anything. It is merely a description of how to emit integers. To get those integers out, we need to run it. This is an important functional theme. We make a clean distinction between the *pure* version of a program and the *impure* part when the program is running, as this is when it may experience side effects. Side effects such as printing to standard out or throwing an exception make the running state *impure*. The paradigm of describing a computation and running only when explicitly told to do so is an advanced, functional process. We will look into this process in Chapter 7.

There are many useful run functions. Here is one example:

Scala

```scala
source.runForEach(i => println(i))
```

As a description of a process, a source can be reused.[3] Let's see an example of taking this source and writing it to a file:

Scala

```scala
source.runWith(FileIO.toPath(Paths.get("numbers.txt"))
```

Flow

In between the `Source` and `Sink` we can have flows. Flows take the incoming data and create a new piece of data based on it. This is instead of mutating the state of the incoming data. Here is an extended example:

Scala

```scala
import akka.actor.ActorSystem
import akka.stream.ActorMaterializer
import akka.stream.scaladsl.{Sink, Source}
import java.io.File

implicit val actorSystem = ActorSystem("system")
implicit val actorMaterializer = ActorMaterializer()

val source = Source(List("test1.txt", "test2.txt", "test3.txt"))
val mapper = Flow[String].map(new File(_))
val existsFilter = Flow[File].filter(_.exists())
val lengthZeroFilter = Flow[File].filter(_.length() != 0)
val sink = Sink.foreach[File](f => println(s"Absolute path: ${f.getAbsolutePath}"))
```

---

3 Unlike, say, an iterator.

```
val stream = source
  .via(mapper)
  .via(existsFilter)
  .via(lengthZeroFilter)
  .to(sink)

stream.run()
```

As we said, a stream in Akka is not executed off the bat; it is initially a description of a stream computation. It has to be *materialized* and that is why we implicitly import the `ActorMaterializer` class. In the sink variable, the `println` does not take place until the line `stream.run()`. That is when the description of the computation turns into an actual computation.

Sink

Let us consider the `Sink` of a stream. If a `source` is where the data comes from, the `Sink` is where the data goes to. A `Sink` is an operator with exactly one input, requesting and accepting data elements, possibly slowing down the upstream producer of elements. This slowing down is known as *backpressure* and the fact that it comes for free with Akka streams is a valuable extra. Some examples:

Scala

```
val source = Source(1 to 10)
val sink = Sink.fold[Int, Int](0)(_ + _)
val sum: Future[Int] = source.runWith(sink)
```

As with a `Source`, a `Sink` is just a description of a computation. The actual value needs to be *materialized* as it is called.

These examples add up the numbers from the `source`.

So we have seen how we can join a `source` to a `Flow` or `Flows` and to a `Sink` to create a stream computation. Akka streams can do a lot more than this. For more on Akka streams, a good place to start is the documentation (*https://oreil.ly/jblSQ*).

More on Streams

Now that we have seen some examples of how streams might be implemented, let's look more fundamentally at streams and how they fit into the functional paradigm.

 It certainly is possible to write streams that mutate state. Beware! This means they are not purely functional streams.

We will focus on purely functional streams. Let us consider them from a more general, theoretical perspective. This is not always how streams are used but it is one way of looking at them that is particularly functional. We will consider a very specific situation. We have a stream S and a sequence of object x_n in the stream where n ranges over the positive integers. So at various times, the stream contains x_1, x_2, x_3, etc. In fact, let us simplify it even more and say that at time n, the stream S contains only one object, namely x_n. Since the subscripts represent time, we are inclined to think of the objects as *streaming* or moving through the stream in time. We are also inclined to think of the x_n objects changing. However, there is another way of thinking about this situation, namely that x_n is an *aspect* of a larger object x. x can exist in various states.

So x has different states. At time n, x is in state x_n. When we look at it this way, we can see x as an unchanging object that exists all at once.

It's not that x_n changes into x_{n+1} but rather x_n and x_{n+1} and every other x_i all exist at the same time to form x. At the code level, we use only immutable data and create new objects x_n in the stream for different values of n. It's a matter of perspective. There is one unchanging object called x that we can write as (x_n). When we think about x, we see it is as a complete, unchanging object. When we think of the stream as containing x_n at time n, it seems to be changing, but this is an illusion based on the fact that we are not looking at x as a completed object.

We have said that it is possible to have streams that mutate state. One has to go through a bit of work to ensure that no state is mutated, but there are some good libraries that take care of this for you. The most popular is called FS2.

FS2: Functional Streams for Scala

In this section, we'll look at streams from a functional perspective.

As it says on the FS2 website (*https://oreil.ly/ykxk5*):

> FS2 is a library for purely functional, effectful, and polymorphic stream processing library in the Scala programming language. Its design goals are compositionality, expressiveness, resource safety, and speed. The name is a modified acronym for Functional Streams for Scala (FSS, or FS2).

FS2 is built upon two functional libraries for Scala: Cats and Cats Effect. To use, simply include the following configuration in your *build.sbt* file:

```
// available for 2.12, 2.13, 3.0
libraryDependencies += "co.fs2" %% "fs2-core" % "<version>"
```

Let's look at a small example of how FS2 works. Note how FS2 uses the *program as description and then run* model. There is a class called IO, from the Cats Effect library, which we will describe in more detail in Chapter 7. For now, think of it as a Future. It will hold a value when the process has completed its action. The variable converter doesn't actually do anything. It merely describes the program. Then when the run function is called, the program actually does what it should do.

```
import cats.effect.{IO, IOApp}
import fs2.{Stream, text}
import fs2.io.file.{Files, Path}

object Converter extends IOApp.Simple {

  val converter: Stream[IO, Unit] = {
    def fahrenheitToCelsius(f: Double): Double =
      (f - 32.0) * (5.0/9.0)

    Files[IO].readAll(Path("testdata/fahrenheit.txt"))
      .through(text.utf8.decode)
      .through(text.lines)
      .filter(s => !s.trim.isEmpty && !s.startsWith("//"))
      .map(line => fahrenheitToCelsius(line.toDouble).toString)
      .intersperse("\n")
      .through(text.utf8.encode)
      .through(Files[IO].writeAll(Path("testdata/celsius.txt")))
  }

  def run: IO[Unit] =
    converter.compile.drain
}
```

The converter object is a Stream and converter.compile runs the stream. drain effectively waits for the stream to run its course. It is essentially blocking until it completes. Each line being called here *modifies* the text by performing some operation and then creating a new piece of text. This code is purely functional. No state is modified, it is simply replaced with a new line that has been processesed in some way. The following is a word count example:

```
def readAndWriteFile(readFrom: String, writeTo: String): Stream[IO, Unit] =
  Stream.resource(Blocker[IO]).flatMap { blocker =>
  val source: Stream[IO, Byte] =
            io.file.readAll[IO](Paths.get(readFrom), blocker, 4096)

  val pipe : Pipe[IO,Byte,Byte] = src =>
    src.through(text.utf8Decode)
    .through(text.lines)
      .flatMap(line => Stream.apply(line.split("\\W+"): _*))
      .fold(Map.empty[String, Int]) {
        (count, word) =>
          count + (word -> (count.getOrElse(word, 0) + 1))
```

```
    }
    .map (_.foldLeft("") {
        case (accumulator, (word, count)) =>
            accumulator + s"$word = $count\n"
      }
    )
    .through(text.utf8Encode)

val sink : Pipe[IO,Byte,Unit] = io.file.writeAll(Paths.get(writeTo), blocker)

source
  .through(pipe)
  .through(sink)
}
```

This example, too, is purely functional. No mutated state anywhere.

Conclusion

The way we approach concurrency in FP is by insuring that as much of our code is immutable as is possible and that we minimize changing state as much as possible.

In addition, we have seen that streaming is also an important part of implementing concurrency in a functional program. Viewing objects as streams allows you to see the entire lifetime of a changing object as a stream that doesn't change at all. Streams are an important tool for handling concurrency.

CHAPTER 7

Where to from Here?

We have seen the various aspects of FP such as immutability, referential transparency, higher order functions, laziness, and pattern matching, and we have seen various methods of employing all these constructs in our code. What is the next level? How do we get there? There are a few ways we can proceed.

Taking the Pure Route

We have emphasized throughout the book that the more of these techniques we employ, "the more functional" our code becomes. But can code be "completely functional"? The answer is "kind of," and we will describe precisely what this means. We call such code "purely functional code" or "pure functional code." I will first deal with some low hanging fruit: `print` statements. There are a number of side effects that occur in most nontrivial programs. For example, writing to a file, printing to the console, opening a socket, throwing an exception. If our code has any of these, it is not purely functional.

What can we do about this? If we cannot keep side effects out of our code completely, at least we can quarantine all the necessary side effects to the outer border, as it were, of the program so it will be perfectly clear to anybody reading the program where the *impure* parts are. I use the phrase *outer border* metaphorically. It is a matter of isolating all the side effects in one part of the program that is easily distinguishable from the rest. We can think of these as the *pure* part of the program and the *impure* part. The impure part is where all the side effects are.

Suppose we want to include the following line in our code:

```
println("Starting up...")
```

This is a side effect. What would isolating this side effect to the outer border of the program look like? To do this, let us create a Scala trait SE (for side effect) with a run method:

```
trait[A] SE(a: A) { def run }
```

The way this works is that we wrap the println statement in this trait. But the expression does not actually print anything:

```
SE(println("starting up"))
```

Think of it as a description of the side effect. It is only when we call its run method that printing occurs. Scala does not actually have a trait like this but in the Cats Effect library for FP in Scala, there is a class just like this. It happens to be a monad and is called IO. Let us see another way to motivate the IO monad that has to do with referential transparency.

Consider the following program:

```
val x = 23
(x, x)
```

Is the previous program the same as the following?

```
(23,23)
```

To find out, we can substitute 23 for each instance of x. When we do this, both programs look like this:

```
(23,23)
```

We can conclude that these two programs are in fact the same.

To substitute a value into instances of a variable, the functions in question must be referentially transparent. To understand this, let us try this same example with a println statement.

```
val x = println("Dude!")
(x, x)
```

Is the preceding code the same program as the following?

```
(println("Dude!"), println("Dude"))
```

No! If you run these two programs, you will see that the first one prints out "Dude!" once, while the second prints out "Dude" twice. We set a variable to a value, found every instance of that variable, and substituted the value for the variable. We would like for the program to be the same after this substitution, but as we see in this example, this is not always true. A function that contains a println is not referentially transparent and substitution will fail.

The IO Monad

What to do? Can we just never use functions that are not referentially transparent?

println, reading from a file, writing to a file, querying a database, deleting a table—of course we can't get rid of these functions. There is a solution, though, and it is a general approach to writing functional programs. The idea is to replace the program with a description or blueprint of the program, which describes exactly what the program should do.

This description will not have any side effects. For example, instead of writing to the console, a side effect, it will state that it has to write to the console without actually writing anything. Then, in addition to the description, we have an interpretation of the program. This is where the actions (or side effects) of the program are carried out. To do this, we can use something called an IO monad. It looks like the following:

```
val x = IO { println("Dude!") }
(x, x)
```

This next program is the same:

```
(IO { println("Dude!")}, IO{ println("Dude!")}
```

Neither of these programs actually print anything. They are descriptions. To get the actual result, the IO monad has a method called unsafeRunSync() (there are other methods with similar names). unsafeRunSync carries out the actual side effect. In this case, it prints "Dude!" to the console. The "unsafe" in the name of the method warns us that we are leaving the world of pure FP and entering the "real world."

```
val x = IO { println("Dude!")}
x.unsafeRunSync()
```

This will print "Dude!" to the console.

Since the IO monad is a monad, it has a map and a flatMap method. So we can do the following:

```
val x = IO { println("Dude!") }

val program: IO[Unit] =
  for {
    _ <- x
    _ <- x
  } yield ()

program.unsafeRunSync()
```

This will print "Dude!" twice to the console.

More on the IO monad

In general, suppose we have a function:

```
doSomething
```

And we have a `for` comprehension like the following:

```
for {
    _  <- doSomething
    _  <- doSomething
} yield ()
```

With the IO monad, if we have referential transparency, we can do the following:

```
val task = doSomething

for {
    _  <- task
    _  <- task
} yield ()
```

We can do this with the IO monad but we cannot do this with `Future`. The IO monad is an important part of the Scala FP picture. This is where `Future` falls short, from the FP perspective.

What about Haskell?

Haskell is a programming language designed by a committee. A group of language designers from academia and industry got together to create what was intended to become a *model* purely FP language. Many other programming languages, both pure and impure, take ideas from Haskell. It acts like a prototype for functional ideas. Haskell, as we have said, is purely functional. If I set x to 3, I can never change it. I can create a variable x like this in Scala, but then I have to use the keyword `val`.

```
val x = 3 // can never be changed
```

In Haskell, I don't need any special keywords—immutability is the default behavior. Haskell, like Scala, has a strong type system. In many ways, it seems to me, Martin Odersky had Haskell in mind when he created Scala. But Odersky was very explicit about his intention that Scala should have both functional aspects and object-oriented aspects. This is the main difference between Haskell and Scala.

For those interested in Haskell but on the Java Virtual Machine (JVM), there is an implementation of it called ETA (*https://eta-lang.org*) that runs on the JVM.

But is Haskell a viable route to take? While used occasionally in industry, it still is more of an academic language, better suited to things like creating other languages.

What can we do if we don't want to go the completely pure route?

Taking the Middle Route

Many of the people reading this book may be interested in pursuing FP, but not necessarily by taking the pure route of Haskell or some other purely FP language.[1]

For you, there is what I am calling the middle route. There are a number of programming languages, like Scala, that allow you many of the benefits of FP without insisting, at every step, that every single idea and construction has to be followed. I will list a few of the more popular choices and say a few words about each.

JVM Languages

Kotlin

From Wikipedia:

> Kotlin is a cross-platform, statically typed, general-purpose programming language with type inference. Kotlin is designed to interoperate fully with Java, and the JVM version of Kotlin's standard library depends on the Java Class Library. Kotlin is similar in many ways to Scala though it has a less complex type system. Interestingly, Kotlin also compiles to JavaScript and to front-end web applications via React. According to Google, Kotlin is the preferred language for Android apps, a distinction previously held for Java.

Some interesting features of Kotlin include:

Extenstion functions
This allows you to add a function to any class. Let's say you want a function that can be called on `Strings` that returns the last character. You could do the following:

```
fun String.lastChar(): Char = get(length - 1)
```

Classes are final by default
In Kotlin, if you want to extend a class, the base class has to be marked open. This default behavior is indicative of the functional tendencies of the language.

Data classes
These are much like Scala's case classes.

Clojure

The history of FP goes much further back than Haskell. In 1958, Lisp came on the scene. Lisp is one of the first high-level programming languages. What is immediately

---

1 Some other purely FP languages include Agda, Idris, Curry, and Miranda.

noteworthy about Lisp is its use of parentheses. Here is a sample of the Scheme dialect of Lisp (there are many dialects of Lisp):

```
(define new-withdraw
  (let ((balance 100))
    (lambda (amount)
      (if (>= balance amount)
          (begin (set! balance (- balance amount))
                 balance)
          "Insufficient funds"))))
```

.NET Languages

F# is an FP language from Microsoft that runs on the .NET platform. I see F# as Microsoft's answer to Scala. F# supports both functional and object-oriented programming. If you are constrained to write code for the .NET platform and want to write functional code, F# is a good choice. There is also a .NET version of Haskell, if you prefer a purely FP language on the .NET platform.

Type Classes

One very important construction in Haskell is type classes. Let us look at how they might be used in Scala.

Upon first seeing type classes, they seem to be a lot like Java interfaces or Scala traits. On further exploration, they are far more powerful. They were introduced into Haskell by their creators, Philip Wadler and Stephen Blott. Type classes are defined by specifying a set of functions or constant names, together with their respective types, that must exist in order for that type to belong to that class. In Haskell, there is no notion of the ordinary class we see in other languages. Type classes are *the* classes.

Type classes give us the capability of ad hoc polymorphism. Let me explain this. First, what is polymorphism? Polymorphism literally means "many shapes." It refers to when the same function name can be applied to arguments of various types. To explore this idea, let's start out with a simple function plus, which adds two integers.

Scala

```
def plus(x: Int, y: Int): Int = x + y
```

Now suppose we want this function to work on strings as well. After all, we can "add" two strings by concatenating them. In Scala, we can simply use overloading:

```
def plus(x: Int, y: Int): Int = x + y
def plus(x: String, y: String): String = x + y
```

Something about this is unsatisfying. The two methods are almost identical and we have to define them separately. There must be a better way! Well, let's try inserting a type parameter and see what that gets us:

```
def plus[A](x: A, y: A): A = //what goes here?
```

The problem is we don't know what an A is, which would inform how to combine them. You might suggest we create a trait called, say, HasPlus, and then require our A to be a subtype of HasPlus. We will write HasPlus like this:

```
trait HasPlus[A] {
    def plus(x: A, y: A): A
}
```

Then, we could write our generic plus function like this:

```
def plus[A <: HasPlus[A]](x: A, y: A): A = plus(x,y)
```

The fact that A <: HasPlus[A] means A will necessarily implement plus. This seems to work. But wait a minute! Int and String don't implement HasPlus, and we can't do anything about that. This is where type classes come into the picture. They will allow us to add functions to preexisting classes. This is part of the power of type classes. Let us see how to proceed.

 Type classes allow us to add functions to already existing classes. This makes them a powerful tool indeed.

Here is the good news. When you think about it, we don't need Int and String to be subtypes of HasPlus, we just need them to be "convertible," in some sense, to HasPlus. What if we implicitly converted them to HasPlus? This is possible using Scala implicits. Let us see how this works:

Scala

```
implicit def intToHasPlus(x: Int): HasPlus[Int] = new HasPlus[Int] {
  override def plus(other: Int) = x + other
}

implicit def stringToAddable(x: String): HasPlus[String] = new HasPlus[String] {
  override def add(other: String) = x + other
}
```

Here, we would like to express that class is *convertible* to a HasPlus. How do we do this? We can use Scala's view-bound construction. This uses the operator <%.

A <: B means A can be converted to B. This looks like this:

```
def plus[A <% HasPlus[A]](x: A, y: A): A = x.plus(y)
```

This states that the plus method takes an object of any type A that can be converted (via implicits) to a HasPlus. With those two implicits defined earlier, we can do this:

```
plus(3,4) // evaluates to 7
plus("Hello", " World") // evaluates to "Hello World"
```

The problem with this construction is that view bounds, the <% construct, have been deprecated since Scala version 2.11. This is where type classes come in. Let us once again consider the method:

```
combine(x: A, y: A): A = ?
```

However, we still don't know how to combine the two values. Let us suppose we have a HasPlus trait that tells us how to add the two elements:

```
trait HasPlus[A] {
    def plus(x: A, y: A): A
}
```

Next, we can add the HasPlus through a second parameter list.[2] We can now construct a HasPlus for both Ints and Strings:

```
object IntHasPlus extends HasPlus[Int] {
  override def plus(x: Int, y: Int) = x + y
}

object StringHasPlus extends HasPlus[String] {
  override def plus(x: String, y: String)= x + y
}
```

Now we can call combine like this:

```
combine(2,3)(intHasPlus)
combine("Hello", " World!")(StringHasPLus)
```

We are almost where we want to be. All we have to do now is make the HasPlus implementations implicit:

```
implicit object IntHasPlus extends HasPlus[Int] {
  override def plus(x: Int, y: Int) = x + y
}

implicit object StringHasPlus extends HasPlus[String] {
  override def plus(x: String, y: String)= x + y
}
```

Then, define combine as follows:

```
def combine[A](x: A, y: A)(implicit hasPlus: HasPlus[A]): A =
  hasPlus.plus(x, y)
```

---

2 See Chapter 2 for second parameter lists.

We can simply call like so:

```
combine(2,3)
combine("Hello World")
```

Now, there happens to be a construct in Scala called a context bounds. I will write down the construct and then under that, I will write what it is syntactic sugar for. First, I must introduce the `implicitly` operator.

```
implicitly[A]
```

This simply pulls an instance of A out of `implicit` scope if it exists. Then we can write:

```
def combine[A : HasPlus](x: A, y: A): A = implicitly[HasPlus[A]].plus(x,y)
```

which stands exactly for this:

```
def combine[A](x: A, y: A)(hasPlus: HasPlus[A]): A = hasPlus.plus(x,y)
```

So we can write the following:

```
def combine[A : HasPlus](x: A, y: A): A = implicitly[HasPlus[A]].plus(x,y)
```

This happens automatically; it's as if there were a second parameter list with an implicit `HasPlus` object. To make it even more natural looking, we do the following in the companion object of `HasPlus`:

```
object HasPlus {
  def apply[A: HasPlus]: Hasplus[A] = implicitly
}
```

Now we can write the following:

```
def combine[A : HasPlus](x: A, y: A): A = HasPlus[A].plus(x,y)
```

This will work for any data type for which there is an implicit implementation of `plus`.

Another example of a type class: A JSON Library

We will write some code to model a simple library that serializes JSON. We will start out with a sealed trait called `Json`:

```
sealed trait Json
```

Then we'll add some classes and an object that extend `Json`:

```
final case class JsObject(get: Map[String, Json]) extends Json
final case class JsString(get: String) extends Json
final case class JsNumber(get: Double) extends Json
final case object JsNull extends Json
```

Next, we will need a way to express a `write` method that does the actual serialization. We can do that with the following trait:

```
trait JsonWriter[A] {
  def write(value: A): Json
}
```

`JsonWriter` is the type class we are building. The other traits/classes/objects are supporting code.

Now we create the implicit implementations. These are called *type class instances*. Let's see what these look like:

```
final case class Person(name: String, email: String)

object JsonWriterInstances {
  implicit val stringWriter: JsonWriter[String] =
    new JsonWriter[String] {
      def write(value: String): Json =
        JsString(value)
    }

  implicit val personWriter: JsonWriter[Person] =
    new JsonWriter[Person] {
      def write(value: Person): Json =
        JsObject(Map(
          "name" -> JsString(value.name),
          "email" -> JsString(value.email)
        ))
    }

  // etc...
}
```

This completes the type class. How do we use it?

What we really want is a method named `toJson`, which serializes an object of type T, for every T for which there is a type class instance. We have one for the case class `Person`. Thus, we can do the following:

```
object Json {
  def toJson[A](value: A)(implicit w: JsonWriter[A]): Json =
    w.write(value)
}
```

Then, we can do this:

```
import JsonWriterInstances._

Json.toJson(Person("Andrea", "andrea@example.com"))
```

This will produce the following output:

```
Map("name" -> JsString("Andrea"), "email" -> JsString("andrea@example.com"))
```

Now suppose we would like to be able to do something like this:

```
Person("Andrea", "andrea@example.com").toJson
```

We want to do this even though there is no toJson method in the Person case class. One of the nice things about type classes is adding methods to already created classes. Here is the code to do this:

```
object JsonSyntax {
  implicit class JsonWriterOps[A](value: A) {
    def toJson(implicit w: JsonWriter[A]): Json =
      w.write(value)
  }
}
```

Now we can do the following:

```
import JsonWriterInstances._
import JsonSyntax._

Person("Andrea", "andrea@example.com").toJson
```

This will give us what we want.

Conclusion

There is no end to what you can do with type classes. To see many more examples, look at the Cats library (*https://oreil.ly/lXxBp*). It has many built-in type classes that are useful in a functional context.

Whether you choose to pursue the pure functional path with a language like Haskell or Scala with the Cats library, or you decide to pursue the middle path with a language like F#, Clojure, C#, Java, or Scala, FP makes things cleaner, clearer, more generic, and more composable.

Scala

Why am I devoting an appendix to one particular programming language? My experience of programming in many languages combined with my experience of FP has taught me that although it is possible to express functional concepts in any language, to one extent or another, some languages lend themselves more naturally to functional thinking and expression.

 While it is possible to express functional concepts in virtually any language, a language that was designed to partially or fully support functional constructs makes it easier to learn and appreciate what FP is all about.

It is for this reason that I have decided to introduce examples in a few different languages, so that you can see how one might go about expressing functional concepts with a variety of tools and capabilities. However, it is my sincere belief that to fully appreciate the beauty and utility of functional concepts, one needs to see them expressed in a language that was designed with these ends in mind.

I could have chosen Haskell, a purely functional language that is in many ways the archetypical functional language, but I thought it best to err on the side of practicality. So I chose Scala, which is a hybrid language. Its designer, Martin Odersky, wanted a language that could produce functional code and object-oriented code equally well.

 Scala is a hybrid language. It was designed to support both the object-oriented and functional paradigms.

There are examples in other languages in the book. However, some of the "most functional" topics will stick to Scala examples mainly because all the code it would take to express these concepts in other languages would take attention away from the book's main goal: to learn how to think functionally without getting bogged down in too much syntax. I would also add (and I should explicitly label this as opinion) that a careful reading of this introduction to Scala will provide another benefit that is perhaps not obvious at first. It will get you started on thinking functionally. The concepts are "built into" the language, as it were.

 If you prefer not to read this introduction to Scala, you can still fruitfully read the book.

Assumptions

I am making a few assumptions about your knowledge of programming. I assume you are familiar with the general concepts you pick up when you have been programming for a while. I assume you know about classes in OOP. I also assume you know what functions are and what methods are. To be clear, I will consider a method to be a function that is associated with a particular class. Otherwise, they are the same. I will assume you know what exceptions are, because almost all programming languages have them. Finally, I assume you are familiar with the usual programming constructs such as for loops, while loops, case statements, etc.

Overview

Let us start by describing the Scala language. Scala is a statically typed language with support for both functional and object oriented programming. It supports pure functions, higher order functions, lazy evaluation, pattern matching, immutability, currying, and a very expressive type system. Let me explain some of these terms:

Statically typed
  This means each piece of data in the language has its own data type that describes what kind of data it is. For example, a string, an integer, or a custom type.

Functional programming
  A style of programming in which we use pure functions, immutable data, and structures from category theory.

Object-oriented programming
  A style of programming that models a domain as a collection of objects, each with its own set of methods or operations it can perform.

Pure functions

A pure function is a function that takes an input and returns an output (and does nothing else). There are no side effects. It does not modify any variables outside the function; it does not write to a file or throw an exception. It merely takes an input and returns an output. If you supply it with the same input, it will return the same output.

Higher order functions

A higher order function is a function that takes other functions as parameters or returns a function.

Lazy evaluation

Lazy evaluation means an expression is evaluated only when it is needed. In general, without lazy evalutation, if a function that is not lazy takes a parameter, then as soon as that function is called, the variable substituted for that parameter is evaluated. If it is lazy, it will not be evaluated until it is needed.

Pattern matching

Pattern matching is like a switch or case statement on steroids. We will investigate this later in the book.

Immutability

Immutability means that something never changes. If a variable x is immutable, then once it is set, it can never be changed.

Type system

This simply refers to the collection of all types in the programming language.

var and val

There are two way to declare a variable in Scala. One is with the keyword var and the other is with the keyword val. var is like a variable in any other language. A var, once declared and set to a value, can be changed at any time. A val, once set, can never be changed. If Martin Odersky, the creator of Scala, had wanted Scala to be a purely functional programming language, he would have had only vals. It is a best practice in Scala to use vals whenever possible and use a var only when it is necessary. One reason a var could be considered necessary is if you want to implement an algorithm in a way that is optimized for performance. This might involve looping through a collection and continually resetting the value of a variable. In general, in good Scala code, `var`s are avoided whenever possible.

```
val x = 3
x = x + 1 // compiler error!

var y = 3
y = y + 1 // compiles
```

Classes and Objects

In Java and object-oriented programming languages generally, an object is an instance of a class. If I write:

Java

```
User user = new User();
```

Then User is a class and user is an instance of that class. This usage holds in Scala too, except there is another meaning of the word *object*. In Scala, object is a keyword that declares a singleton. If I write the following:

Scala

```
object User {
    def getUserName = ???
}
```

This code creates a class named User behind the scenes and creates an instance of the class. However, only one instance is ever allowed.

The ??? is an expression to fill in some code that is not complete but you still want the code to compile.

So we could write:

Scala

```
User.getUserName
```

and this would evaluate to whatever this user's username is.

Functions

Let's look at some simple functions in Scala.

Scala

```
def square(n: Int): Int = n * n
```

Notice how the type of the parameter is structured with a colon and then the type. Also, the return type follows a colon. In Scala, the compiler can infer the type of a variable in many cases. When that is the case, Scala allows you to leave the type out. For example:

```
def square(n: Int) = n * n
```

The compiler has no way of inferring the type of the argument n; arguments always need a type. As a general rule, however, it is a good idea to include types, especially in the case of public-facing APIs, to give the user of the API a clearer picture.

Here are some other ways to express the square function.

```scala
def square = (n: Int) => n * n
```

The right side is an anonymous function.

This can also be a `val`.

```scala
val square = (n: Int) => n * n
```

The difference between these is that a `val` is evaluated when it is defined and a `def` is evaluated when it is called.

Functions that Return Functions

Let's say we want a function that creates a function that adds a fixed number to its argument. In Scala, we can do the following:

```scala
def addA(a: Int) = (n: Int) => n + a
```

To be clearer, we can add the return type of `addA`.

```scala
def addA(a: Int): Int => Int = (n: Int) => n + a
```

Case Classes

Case classes are powerful and a great example of the sort of useful and efficient constructions you see in Scala. They have additional structures and you can make additional presuppositions about them. A case class does not need the keyword `new` before it, and it comes with `equals`, `hashCode`, `toString`, and `copy` functions, to name a few. We can define a case class as follows:

Scala

```scala
case class Document(id: Int, title: String: numOfPages: Int)
```

Then, we can use it as follows:

Scala

```scala
val doc = Document(1,"Earnings", 35)
```

If we want to copy `doc` but change the number of pages, we can do the following:

Scala

```scala
val newDoc = doc.copy(numOfPages = 37)
```

An important point about case classes is that when they are tested for equality, they are compared by the fields, not references. So, if we have the following:

Scala

```
val doc1 = Document(3, "My Vacation", 10)
val doc2 = Document(3, "My Vacation", 10)
```

Then doc1 == doc2 will evaluate to true, even though they are two distinct instances of the class Document. We can express this by saying that equality is *by value*.

If a case class is an object and not a class, we call it a case object.

When we come to pattern matching, we will see a particularly nice use of case classes in Scala.

Declaring Functions

All arguments to a function need a type associated with them. How does one declare the type of a function? Let us look at some examples.

Scala

```
f: Int => Int
```

This is a function that takes an Int and returns an Int. This resembles the way mathematicians write a function. Here is another one.

```
f: (User, Int) => Double
```

This function takes an object of type tuple of a User and an Int and returns a Double.

Currying

In a purely functional program, one that makes no compromises, functions with one argument are considered superior to functions that take multiple arguments. You can always create a class with the multiple arguments as fields and then have a function that takes an object of that class and returns a variable. But this is kind of kludgy. Scala provides a better approach. Currying is a way of transforming a function of multiple arguments into a function of one argument. Let's see how this works; suppose we start off with a function that takes two Ints and returns an Int.

Scala

```
def f(a: Int, b: Int): Int = a + b
```

Let's see how currying transforms this function. We write each argument with its own parentheses, like so:

```
def f(a: Int)(b: Int) = a + b
```

How do we interpret this definition? `f(a)` takes an `Int` and returns a function that takes an `Int` and returns an `int`.

```
f(3)(4)
```

`f(3)` is a function that takes an `Int` and adds 3 to it.

Anonymous Functions

Let us consider a function that takes two `Int`s and adds them together. The basic way of writing this in Scala is the following:

Scala

```
def sum(m: Int, n: Int): Int = m + n
```

Let's see how to write this without naming it.

```
(m: Int, n: Int) => m + n
```

We can assign this to a variable like so:

```
val f = (m: Int, n: Int) => m + n
```

Higher Order Functions

A higher order function is simply a function that takes other functions as arguments or returns a function. We will look at some examples and then we will see how this concept promotes abstraction.

```
def apply(f: Int => Int, a: Int) = f(a)
```

This function takes a function from `Int` to `Int` and an `Int` and applies that function to that `Int`.

What about a more complex example that returns a function?

```
def f(a: Int): Int => Int = (n: Int) => n + a
```

This function takes an `Int` and returns a function that takes an `Int` and adds `a` to it.

Here is an example with currying.

```
def f(a: Int)(b: Int): Int = (m: Int) => a * b + m
```

How do higher order functions promote abstraction? The key is that they give us the ability to pass in a function that represents a particular chunk of functionality. Suppose we have a situation where we are doing a computation, and the algorithm we use depends on the value of a variable x. Say there are three algorithms `alg1`, `alg2`, and `alg3`. These are three functions. Then we could do something like this:

```
if (x <10)
    f(alg1)
```

```
    else if (x < 20)
        f(alg2)
    else
        f(alg3)
```

Another way higher order functions can promote abstraction is by creating a class that takes a parameter that is a function:

```
class Method(s: Strategy)
```

Here, Strategy is an alias for a function. In Scala, we can do this as follows:

```
type Strategy = (n: Double) => Double
```

Essentially, this allows us to create a class and specify a chunk of functionality, which in this case represents a strategy for solving some problem.

The general idea is that higher order functions allow us to pass around functionality instead of just simple data types like Int or String.

Pattern Matching

Pattern matching is like a switch statement on steroids. The set of things you can match against is much greater than just Ints or Strings. Let's look at some examples.

First, we reproduce a simple match on integers. This is essentially the usual switch statement.

Scala

```
def f(n: Int): Int = 3

f(2) match {
    case 1 => "no"
    case 2 => "no"
    case 3 => "yes"
    case _ println("value not found")
}
```

This expression would evaluate to the string "yes". Let me emphasize here that this pattern matching construction is an expression that evaluates to a value. We could actually store this in a variable like so:

```
val x = f(2) match {
    case 1 => "no"
    case 2 => "no"
    case 3 => "yes"
    case _ println("no match")
}
```

The value x would then contain the string "yes". The case _ matches the case when none of the other values are matched.

Let's look at some other examples:

```scala
import scala.util.Random

val x: Int = Random.nextInt(10)

x match {
  case 0 => "zero"
  case 1 => "one"
  case 2 => "two"
  case _ => "other"
}
```

I mentioned earlier that case classes were particularly useful in pattern matching.

```scala
case class User(firstName: String, age: Int)

val user = User("Katherine", 26)

user match {
    case User(_, 25) => "not a match"
    case User("Katherine", _) => "a match!"
    case User(_, 26) => "a match"
}
```

The pattern matching expression can "see into" the fields and match against them. It even works with embedded objects.

```scala
case class Name(first: String, last: String)
case class User(name: Name, age: Int)

User(Name("John", "Smith"), 77) match {
    case User(Name(_, "Smith"), _) => "A Smith!"
}
```

You can add boolean expressions to refine the match.

```scala
case class Name(first: String, last: String)
case class User(name: Name, age: Int)

val user = User(Name("Katherine","Smith"), 26)

user match {
  case User(Name(_, last), _) if (last(0).toString.toUpperCase=="S") =>
      println("a match!")
}
```

It is also possible to match on type.

```scala
abstract class Device
case class Phone(model: String) extends Device {
  def screenOff = "Turning screen off"
}
case class Computer(model: String) extends Device {
```

```
    def screenSaverOn = "Turning screen saver on..."
}

def goIdle(device: Device) = device match {
  case p: Phone => p.screenOff
  case c: Computer => c.screenSaverOn
}
```

As you can see, pattern matching is a powerful construction.

Traits

It's tempting to say traits are like Java interfaces but that you can implement some (or all) of the methods. (Java 8 allows default and static methods to be implemented.) This characterization would not be totally false, but it is incomplete. Traits offer so much more than this.

Let us start with the simplest possible `trait`.

```
trait Printable
```

Say we are creating a class called `Document` and we want to make clear that `Documents` have a method called `print`. We can do this:

```
class Document extends Printable
```

Since `Printable` has no methods, we don't need to have a method called `print` in `Document`. The preceding declaration is a bit misleading, but it's just meant as an example of the simplest `trait`. To ensure there is a `print` method, we do the following:

```
trait Printable {
    def print: Unit
}

class Document extends Printable
```

In this case, the compiler will enforce that there is a `print` method in `Document`.

A class can extend any number of traits. Suppose we have another `trait` called `Scannable`. How would we specify that `Document` extends both traits?

```
trait Printable {
    def print: Unit
}

trait Scannable {
    def scan: Unit
}

class Document extends Printable with Scannable
```

We can have as many `with` clauses as we want.

 Let us be clear that a trait can have both implemented and unimplemented methods.

Distinguishing Abstract Classes and Traits

Like Java, Scala also has abstract classes. Both an abstract class and a trait can have implemented and nonimplemented methods. Also, neither can be instantiated. So what are the differences?

First of all, perhaps the main difference is that a class can extend only one abstract class (or concrete class, for that matter). Scala does *not* have multiple inheritance of classes. It does have multiple inheritance of traits.

Another rather interesting difference is that you can add a `trait` to an instance of a `class` in Scala but you cannot add an abstract `class` to an instance. With a `trait`, this would look like:

```
trait Loggable
class Document

val d = new Document with Loggable
```

In this case, it is not true that all `Documents` are `Loggable`, only that this particular one is (as any other instances created in this way will be).

Another difference is that classes can take parameters in their definitions. For example:

```
class Person(name: String) {
    //other stuff
}
```

In this example, the `class` itself functions as a constructor and has a constructor parameter. Traits cannot do this (since they cannot be instantiated anyway).

Abstract classes are completely interoperable with Java code when they don't have any constructor parameters. Traits are completely interoperable with Java code when they don't have any implemented methods.

Lazy Evaluation

An expression in Scala is said to be evaluated lazily if it evaluated when it is needed, not immediately. For example, suppose we have a function `f` that carries out a time consuming computation. Also, we have another function `g` that takes `f` as an argument. For non-lazy expressions, when you call a function, the first thing Scala does is evaluate all of its arguments. Now defs cannot be lazy, only vals. Let's consider the following code:

```
val h = longRunningComputation
g(h)
```

In this case, since h is not marked lazy, as soon as g is called, h will be evaluated (and will take a lot of time). Now consider this code:

```
lazy val h = longRunningComputation
g(h)
```

In *this* case, when g is called, h won't be called until it is needed. lazy is useful sometimes in improving a program's performance. Elsewhere in the book, we see some other kinds of benefits of using lazy evaluation.

Type Parameters

In Scala, a list of Strings can be defined as follows:

Scala

```
val lst: List[String] = List("abc", "def")
```

List by itself is not a type. It is what is called a *type constructor*. We see these elsewhere in the book. The type constructor List becomes a type when combined with another type. The following are types:

```
List[Int], List[String], List[User] etc
```

The Option Type

It is a common principle among Scala developers that null is something to be avoided. So, what do we use in its place? The Option type has two subtypes, Some and None. Some wraps a value and None is a standalone type. Let us see an example. A typical example of when a null might be used in another programming language is a function that takes a String that represents a username and returns a user object if it exists for that username. In Java, for example, you might return a null if the username is not found. Here is how we might do this in Scala:

```
def getUser(userName: String): Option[User] = ???
```

If no user is found, the function can return None.

If a user is found, it will return Some(user) where user is the instance of the User object associated with userName.

Options go well with pattern matching. Here is an example:

Scala

```scala
val userName = "victoria2002"
getUser(userName) match {
    case Some(user) => //do something with user
    case None => //Display message to user
}
```

Future

The future F is another type constructor. As with List and Option, a future F by itself is not a type, but rather a type constructor. If we give it a type parameter T, we get the type F[T]. But what is a future? An ordinary variable holds a value *now*. A future will hold a value at some point in the future. It is particularly useful for setting the value of some intensive, long-running computation. For example, let f be a function defined on the whole numbers Z, which typically takes one minute to complete. If we set an ordinary variable to the value of this function, say:

```scala
val x = f(5)
```

The thread running this code will halt for one minute. This could involve halting the UI for one minute. This is catastrophic for a program. Now, let's consider using a future. We can do this:

```scala
val fut: Future[Int] = f(5)
```

The code will immediately run the next line of code even though fut does not yet hold the value of f(5). The next logical question is, "How do we know when the value is complete and then how do we get the value?" Good question. The Future class has a method called onComplete. We can do something like the following:

```scala
val fut: Fut[Int] = f(5)
fut onComplete {
    case Success(n) => println(s"The answer is $n")
    case Failure(ex) => println(ex.getMessage)
}
```

In addition to onComplete, we can use a number of higher order functions with futures. For example:

```scala
val s: Future[String] = getName(id)
```

where getName is a function that gets a name with a long running computation. We could then do something like:

```scala
s.map( s => s.toUpperCase)
```

When the future completes, this expression will evaluate to something like:

```scala
Future("JOSEPH")
```

To use the Future class, we need two imports. One is:

```
import scala.concurrent.Future
```

and the other is:

```
import ExecutionContext.Implicits.global
```

This latter import brings in something called an ExecutionContext. While we will not delve into ExecutionContexts, you can think of it, roughly speaking, as a thread pool. It's an environment in which computations can run asynchronously. Futures are very popular in Scala programming because they allow for asynchronous computation. In pure, FP programs, they are sometimes frowned upon because they go against the principle of referential transparency, which we discussed in Chapter 1. One possible replacement for futures, which *is* purely functional, is the IO monad, discussed in Chapter 7.

Some Key Higher Order Functions

The most important higher order functions to know are map, flatten, and flatMap.

map

The map function takes a collection of objects and a function f defined on those objects and returns a new collection where the _n_th object in the collection is that object transformed by f. Here are some examples.

Scala

```
def square(n: Int): Int = n * n
List(1,2,3,4,5).map(square)
```

This returns the collection:

```
List(1,4,9,16,25)
```

Here is a function that takes a list of numbers, squares each one, and adds all the squares. Notice how concise the expression is:

Scala

```
def squareAndSum(lst: List[Int]): Int = lst.map(square).sum
```

What if we have a list of something that is not a simple type? For example, Options.

```
def getUser(userName: String): Option[User] = ???
val names: List[String] = List("username1", "username2", "username3")
names.map(getUser)
```

This will evaluate to something like:

```
List(None, Some(user1), Some(user2))
```

flatten

There is a method in Scala called `flatten`, which can be useful. Consider the following:

```
names.map(getUser).flatten
```

This will evaluate to:

```
List(user1, user2)
```

The beauty of this method is that it flattens the `Some` instances and throws away the Nones.

flatMap

If you `map` a collection and then `flatten` it, there is another method equivalent to this called `flatMap`.

Let's look at the `flatten` example again and see how it looks expressed with `flatMap`.

```
names.map(getUser).flatten //This evaluates to List(user1,user2)
names.flatMap(getUser)  //This also evaluates to List(user1,user2)
```

`flatMap` plays a huge role in FP.

Some Other Important Higher Order Functions

foldLeft

`foldLeft` is defined on collections and takes a starting element and a binary operation defined on pairs of elements from the collection. It's a way of taking an operation used to combine two elements and applying it to all of the elements of the collection. Here are some examples.

Scala

```
List(1,2,3,4,5).foldLeft((n: Int, m: Int) => n + m) //Evaluates to 10
```

Incidentally, this can also be expressed as follows:

```
List(1,2,3,4,5).foldLeft(_ + _)
```

This uses a shortcut, `_ + _`, for the anonymous function.

```
List("abc", "def", "ghi").foldLeft(_ + _)  //Evaluates to "abcdefghi"
```

Going back to this:

```
List(1,2,3,4,5).foldLeft(0)(_+_)
```

We can replace + with any arbitrary function f that takes two integers and combines them. For example:

```
def f(n: Int,m: Int): Int = 2 * m + n
List(1,2,3,4,5).foldLeft(1)(_ + _)  //Evaluates to 31
```

foldLeft starts on the left of the collection. There is a foldRight, too. If the collection is commutative, foldLeft is equal to foldRight.

filter

filter is a higher order function defined on collections that takes a predicate, that is, a function that returns a Boolean, and filters out all the elements of the collection that do not satisfy the predicate. Here are some examples:

```
def isEven(n: Int): Boolean = (n % 2 == 0)

List(1,2,3,4,5).filter(isEven)  //Evaluates to List(2,4)

def startsWithA(s: String): Boolean = (s.length > 0 && s(0)toUpperCase == 'A')
List("abc", "def", "ghi", "axy").
        filter(startsWithA) //Evaluates to List("abc", "axy")
```

Conclusion

Scala is a particularly good language for learning FP. While it allows for most of the functional constructs we would want, it also allows you to use object-oriented code in your programs. On top of that, it has a very concise and clear syntax that makes (well-written) Scala code easy to read.[1]

---

1 These are opinions, clearly labeled as such. But they are based on my experience with FP and many different programming languages.

Index

About the Author

Jack Widman started his professional life as a mathematician in academia. He studied and taught the intricacies of the mathematical theory of pseudo-compact topological groups, as well as teaching calculus and discrete math courses. At the suggestion of some friends, he decided to try out programming and see if it resonated with him. It is now 24 years later, and Jack has been designing and writing code ever since. With a PhD in mathematics and 24 years of software industry experience, Jack conceived of the idea to write a book on functional programming, a subject with deep mathematical roots, and this book you have in your hands is the result. In his spare time, Jack enjoys reading, writing, and learning all about cybersecurity.

Colophon

The animal on the cover of *Learning Functional Programming* is a bioluminescent octopus (*Stauroteuthis syrtensis*), also known as a glowing sucker octopus. These small cephalopods are found in the Atlantic Ocean, typically near the edge of the continental shelf along the eastern coast of the United States. They have been observed at depths of up to 4,000 meters (almost two and a half miles!) and prefer water temperatures near 38 degrees Fahrenheit.

The bioluminescent octopus has translucent red-brown skin, which provides camouflage in the cold dark water near the ocean floor. Its soft mantle is 2 to 4 inches long and surrounded by 8 arms of varying lengths, the longest of which is about 14 inches. The arms are joined by two webs that extend two-thirds of the way down from the mantle, giving the glowing sucker octopus the appearance of an open umbrella or bell and allowing it to move its arms without compromising this shape. Researchers have mostly encountered this octopus in this bell-like posture with its arms and web extended outward, but it can also propel itself by contracting the web to expel water like a jellyfish. Each arm is lined with 40 to 50 suckers, but unlike other species of octopus, these do not have adhesive qualities. Instead, they function as light-producing organs that emit a blue-green glow for up to five minutes. This octopus is one of only a few species to exhibit bioluminescence, which could be used to attract prey or deter predators.

Because it spends so much of its time near the bottom of the ocean, the behavior and diet of the glowing sucker octopus has been difficult to observe. Scientists have not yet found a juvenile specimen, so little is known about their development and lifespan, but they are believed to lay around 900 eggs at a time. Examination of preserved specimens suggests that they may eat small crustaceans like copepods, and their bell-shaped web could be used to capture zooplankton.

The IUCN has not been able to classify this species due to a lack of data; while some studies indicate that bioluminescent octopuses have been injured by fishing trawls, the depths of their oceanic habitat may offer some protection from other human threats like climate change and pollution. Many of the animals on O'Reilly covers are endangered; all of them are important to the world.

The cover illustration is by Karen Montgomery, based on a black and white engraving from *The Cephalopods of the North-Eastern Coast of America*. The cover fonts are Gilroy Semibold and Guardian Sans. The text font is Adobe Minion Pro; the heading font is Adobe Myriad Condensed; and the code font is Dalton Maag's Ubuntu Mono.

O'REILLY®

Learn from experts.
Become one yourself.

Books | Live online courses
Instant Answers | Virtual events
Videos | Interactive learning

Get started at oreilly.com.

Lightning Source UK Ltd.
Milton Keynes UK
UKHW031840310822
408135UK00005B/8

9 781098 111755